Contribut

A TWO

©2021. Pu
under licence from West Ham United FC.

ISBN: 978-1-914588-06-8

Every effort has been made to ensure the accuracy
of information within this publication but the publishers
cannot be held responsible for any errors or omissions.
Views expressed are those of the author and do not
necessarily represent those of the publishers or the
football club. All rights reserved.

PICTURE CREDITS: Action Images, Alamy,
Griffiths Photographers, Shutterstock.

WEST HAM UNITED
LONDON

2021/22 HAMMERS
OFFICIAL YEARBOOK

CONTENTS

Fixtures 2021/22	6
West Ham United's European Champions	8
Hammer of the Year	10
Pre-Season	12
Goal of the Year	16
The Boys of 1964	18
Hey Ref!	20
Premier League Squad 2021/22	22
2020/21 Review	44
The Boys of 1975	50
Classic Fan'tastic	52
Rewind Quiz of the Year	54
Premier League Key Players	56
The Boys of 1986	62
PL2 Squad 2021/22	64
Premier League Quiz	70
Academy Squad 2021/22	72
Fast Forward Predictions	76
WHU Women 2021/22	78
The Boys of 2005	80
Quiz Answers	82

WEST HAM UNITED LONDON

2021

AUGUST 2021

Sunday	15	Newcastle United	A	
Monday	**23**	**Leicester City**	**H**	
Saturday	**28**	**Crystal Palace**	**H**	

SEPTEMBER 2021

Saturday	11	Southampton	A	
Thursday	16	Dinamo Zagreb	A	Europa League
Sunday	**19**	**Manchester United**	**H**	
Wednesday	22	Manchester United	A	EFL Cup 3
Saturday	25	Leeds United	A	
Thursday	**30**	**Rapid Vienna**	**H**	Europa League

OCTOBER 2021

Sunday	3	Brentford*	H	
Sunday	17	Everton	A	
Thursday	**21**	**Genk**	**H**	Europa League
Sunday	**24**	**Tottenham Hotspur**	**H**	
Wednesday	**27**	**Manchester City**	**H**	EFL Cup 4
Sunday	31	Aston Villa	A	

NOVEMBER 2021

Thursday	4	Genk	A	Europa League
Sunday	**7**	**Liverpool**	**H**	
Saturday	20	Wolverhampton Wanderers	A	
Thursday	25	Rapid Vienna	A	Europa League
Sunday	28	Manchester City	A	

DECEMBER 2021

Wednesday	**1**	**Brighton & Hove Albion**	**H**	
Saturday	**4**	**Chelsea**	**H**	
Thursday	**9**	**Dinamo Zagreb**	**H**	Europa League
Saturday	11	Burnley*	A	
Tuesday	14	Arsenal	A	
Saturday	**18**	**Norwich City**	**H**	
W/C	20			EFL Cup QF
Sunday	**26**	**Southampton**	**H**	
Tuesday	28	Watford	A	

PREMIER LEAGUE FIXTURES

Please note all fixtures are subject to change.
*These fixtures are subject to change due to our participation in the UEFA Europa League the preceding Thursday.

2022

WEST HAM UNITED LONDON

JANUARY 2022

Saturday	1	Crystal Palace	A	
W/C	3			EFL Cup SF1
Saturday	8			FA Cup 3
W/C	10			EFL Cup SF2
Saturday	15	Leeds United	H	
Saturday	22	Manchester United	A	

FEBRUARY 2022

Saturday	5			FA Cup 4
Tuesday	8	Watford	H	
Saturday	12	Leicester City	A	
Saturday	19	Newcastle United	H	
Saturday	26	Wolverhampton Wanderers	H	
Sunday	27			EFL Cup Final

MARCH 2022

Wednesday	2			FA Cup 5
Saturday	5	Liverpool	A	
Saturday	12	Aston Villa	H	
Saturday	19	Tottenham Hotspur	A	FA Cup QF

APRIL 2022

Saturday	2	Everton	H	
Saturday	9	Brentford	A	
Saturday	16	Burnley	H	FA Cup SF
Saturday	23	Chelsea	A	
Sunday	30	Arsenal	H	

MAY 2022

Saturday	7	Norwich City	A	
Saturday	14			FA Cup Final
Sunday	15	Manchester City	H	
Sunday	22	Brighton & Hove Albion	A	

BARONESS BRADY, KATHY PETERS, ROBERTA MOORE, SIR GEOFF HURST AND DAVID GOLD

The new bronze statue pays tribute to Bobby Moore, Geoff Hurst and Martin Peters plus their teammates who contributed to the club's memorable 1965 European Cup Winners' Cup triumph.

The club's supporters were involved and supported this project after it was decided that the club's original Champions' Statue would remain at the junction of Barking Road and Green Street, adjacent to the club's former home at the Boleyn Ground.

Continued supporter consultation and feedback provided a clear and widespread view from the start of the process to honour the club's rich heritage at the Boleyn Ground and also reflect that at its new home.

Furthermore, any design should focus on the club's three famous sons of the 60s - Moore, Hurst and Peters, who all came through the famous Academy of Football to reach the very pinnacle of the game in 1966, when they led England to World Cup Final glory against West Germany at Wembley.

Additionally, to ensure West Ham United's own greatest achievement at Wembley is also recognised, the lifesize -and-a-quarter bronze statue depicts the three World Cup heroes lifting the European Cup Winners' Cup trophy in 1965, commemorating a performance that catapulted the club onto the world stage after two second-half goals from Alan Sealey saw the Hammers overcome German side TSV Munich 1860.

The formal title of the statue, which is located at Champions Place on the north-east corner of the stadium, is 'West Ham United's European Champions'. The names of the full triumphant team, as well as manager Ron Greenwood, are also immortalised on the plinth of the statue to truly capture a collective and historic success.

Ahead of supporters seeing the statute for the first time prior to the Hammers' 2-0 Europa League victory over Rapid Vienna on 30 September, the official unveiling took place a day earlier with Sir Geoff Hurst, Roberta Moore - daughter of Bobby - and Martin Peters' wife Kathy all fittingly in attendance.

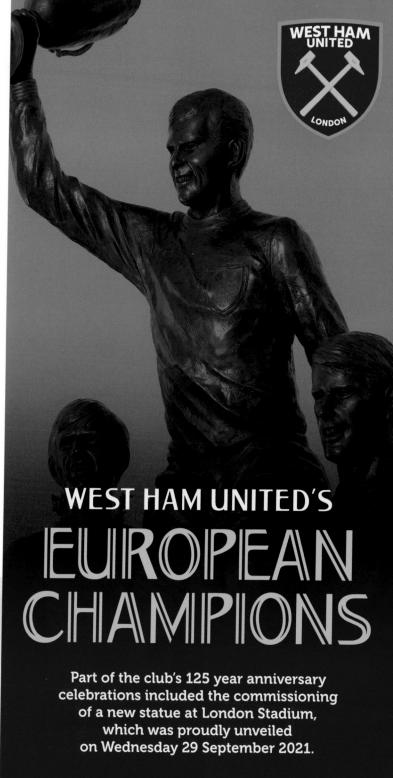

WEST HAM UNITED'S
EUROPEAN CHAMPIONS

Part of the club's 125 year anniversary celebrations included the commissioning of a new statue at London Stadium, which was proudly unveiled on Wednesday 29 September 2021.

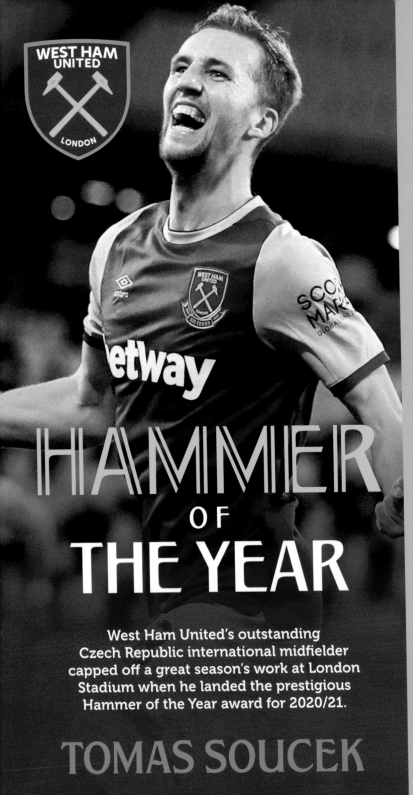

HAMMER OF THE YEAR

West Ham United's outstanding Czech Republic international midfielder capped off a great season's work at London Stadium when he landed the prestigious Hammer of the Year award for 2020/21.

TOMAS SOUCEK

The covid-19 pandemic may have prevented the West Ham faithful from watching games in person, but when it came to casting their votes for the top performing Hammer, they knew only too well what they had seen while watching from home.

Throughout the campaign, 26-year-old Soucek was influential all over the pitch as the Irons finished sixth in the Premier League, setting records for points, wins and away victories.

Soucek was an ever-present in the top-flight, starting and finishing all 38 matches, illustrating his resilience and determination to help his team.

The Czech certainly made good use of his time on the pitch - ending the campaign as the club's joint-leading scorer with ten goals, alongside Michail Antonio, and winning more aerial battles than any other Premier League player. He also led the Hammers in a host of other statistical categories - shots, tackles and interceptions - and ranked second in passes and clearances.

First introduced by the West Ham United Supporters' Club in 1958, the Hammer of the Year award has been won by some of the greatest players in the club's history, including Bobby Moore, Geoff Hurst, Billy Bonds, Trevor Brooking, Tony Cottee and Paolo Di Canio.

The popular Soucek, who becomes the second Czech to be voted Hammer of the Year after goalkeeper Ludek Miklosko in 1991, first collected the trophy at the virtual 2020/21 Player Awards.

"Thank you!" said a smiling Soucek.

"I appreciate it because this season was incredible for me and I just hope that everyone enjoyed it with me, and I hope we can carry on. I really appreciate this prize."

Ahead of the Hammers' opening home game of the new 2021/22 Premier League season, Soucek was given the opportunity to show off his trophy for a second time and on this occasion in front of a capacity crowd at London Stadium when he received the richly-deserved acclaim of the West Ham supporters prior to the 4-1 victory over Leicester City.

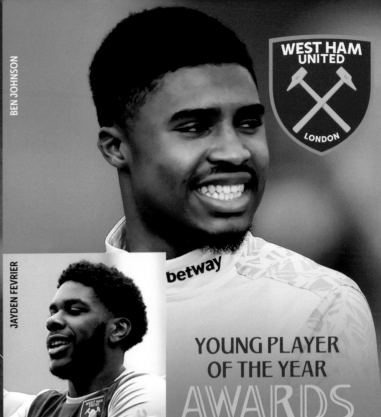

JAYDEN FEVRIER

BEN JOHNSON

YOUNG PLAYER OF THE YEAR AWARDS

Attack-minded full-back Ben Johnson was voted the Hammers' Young Player of the Year for 2020/21 with Jayden Fevrier picking up the Dylan Tombides Award, given to the outstanding Academy scholar.

Johnson's honour came on the back of a season in which he made 20 first-team appearances and scored his first senior goal - in the 2-2 home draw with Brighton & Hove Albion. It represented a real breakthrough for the 21-year-old, who featured at right-back, left-back and higher up the pitch too.

Meanwhile, 18-year-old midfielder Fevrier was a star performer in the under-18s run to the fifth round of the FA Youth Cup, scoring three times in two outings, including two in the dramatic 3-3 draw at Luton Town, before dispatching his penalty in the 4-2 shootout success which followed.

With a further three goals across 19 appearances in the under-18 Premier League South, Premier League 2 Division 1 and the Papa John's Trophy, Fevrier made his mark as one of the Academy's outstanding prospects.

Fevrier collected the trophy named in honour of the late West Ham United and Australia under-23 forward Dylan Tombides, who tragically passed away at the age of 20 in April 2014.

11

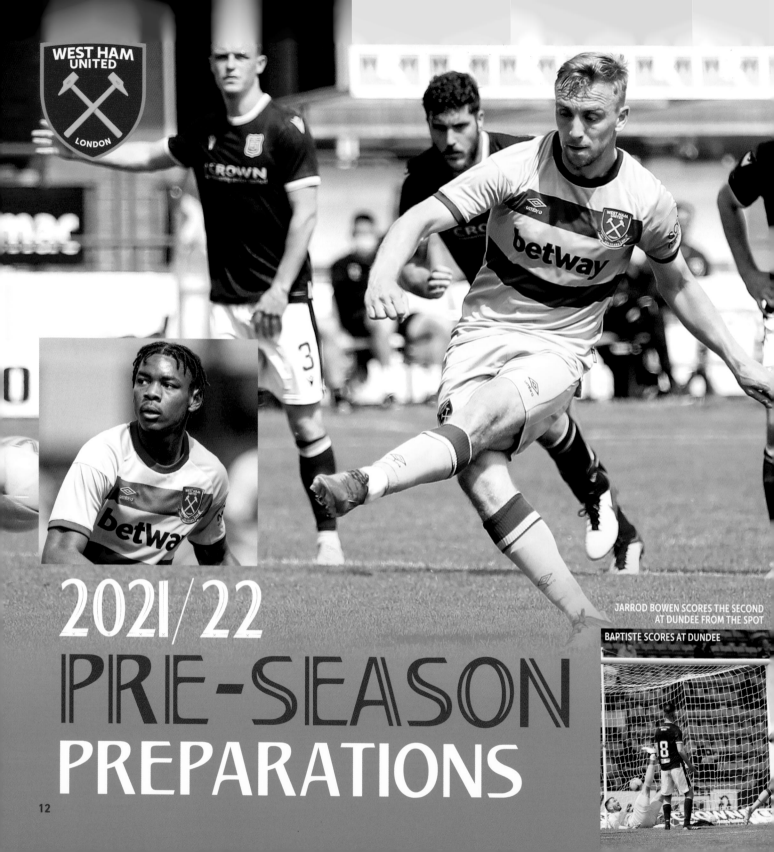

WEST HAM UNITED
LONDON

2021/22
PRE-SEASON
PREPARATIONS

JARROD BOWEN SCORES THE SECOND
AT DUNDEE FROM THE SPOT

BAPTISTE SCORES AT DUNDEE

With the Hammers' 2021/22 Premier League campaign kicking-off away to Newcastle United on Sunday 15 August 2021 - manager David Moyes, his staff and the players were all solely focused on using their pre-season schedule to ensure they were fully prepared for that first whistle of the new season.

Once the players reported back to the training ground following their brief summer breaks, everything was geared-up to making sure the squad would hit the ground running when they stepped out at St James' Park.

The ongoing covid-19 pandemic resulted in this pre-season being drastically different to a number of its predecessors. With overseas travel proving a continual challenge, there was no foreign training camp or pre-season tournament, but the Hammers did manage to schedule in six pre-season friendly fixtures ahead of the Betway Cup match against Atalanta which preceded the big kick-off in the north east.

After a number of tough training sessions, West Ham United returned to action on Friday 9 July when they began their preparations for the new season with a trip to face Scottish Premiership side Dundee at Dens Park.

The home side looked set to claim the Hammers' scalp when they led 2-0 thanks to goals at the start of each half from Charlie Adam and Paul McMullan, but West Ham came roaring back and a quickfire double from Jamal Baptiste and Jarrod Bowen ensured their week-long training camp in St Andrews would end on a positive note.

With the Hammers' international players still yet to return to pre-season training at this juncture, David Moyes had a blend of youth and experience at his disposal at the Kilmac Stadium.

Next up was an assignment far closer to home when West Ham and Leyton Orient battled their way to a 0-0 draw in a pre-season friendly at the Breyer Group Stadium on Tuesday 13 July. On a night of few chances, the senior players on show including Aaron Cresswell, Mark Noble, Michail Antonio, Angelo Ogbonna and Darren Randolph got a valuable 90 minutes in their legs.

Xande Silva and Michail Antonio both came close to breaking the east-London deadlock for David Moyes' men in the closing stages, only to be denied by home goalkeeper Sam Sargeant on both occasions, as the teams had to settle for a share of the spoils.

With the club involved in two friendlies on the night - a second team managed by Stuart Pearce was simultaneously in action at Northampton Town. And it was in that match at Sixfields Stadium that the Hammers registered their first win of the pre-season, edging past the Cobblers with a 2-1 win.

MICHAIL ANTONIO IN ACTION AT LEYTON ORIENT

WEST HAM
UNITED
LONDON

JARROD BOWEN ON THE ATTACK V NORTHAMPTON TOWN

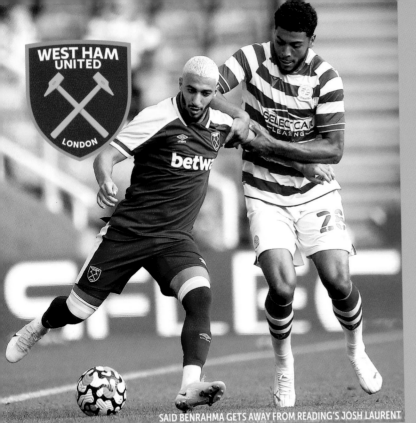

SAID BENRAHMA GETS AWAY FROM READING'S JOSH LAURENT

BENRAHMA CELEBRATES SCORING AT CELTIC WITH PABLO FORNALS

The Hammers were quick off the mark against their League Two opponents and went ahead inside two minutes when the lively Jarrod Bowen's right-wing cross was shinned into the top corner of his own net by home defender Sid Nelson.

Craig Dawson then headed wide as West Ham continued to pile the pressure on the home team. Pearce's side went 2-0 up on 13 minutes when a slick piece of interplay ended with captain Manuel Lanzini teeing up Conor Coventry and the Republic of Ireland under-21 international finished accurately from outside the penalty area. The Cobblers pulled a goal back through Sam Hoskins before half-time, with the right-winger converting Mitch Pinnock's low cross on 29 minutes.

On Wednesday 21 July, the team were back in action and put three past Championship side Reading at the Select Car Leasing Stadium to earn their second pre-season victory in a row.

David Moyes' Irons were on top from the very opening moments of the game and would have enjoyed a greater lead than 1-0 at half time, were it not for inspired goalkeeping from Reading's Rafael.

A fortuitous own-goal by Jeriel Dorsett eventually granted the Hammers the lead, and with the West Ham manager able to introduce a full raft of substitutes in a slower-paced second half, Academy graduate Ben Johnson set up Conor Coventry for a tap-in before adding a third himself with a superb slaloming run in the closing stages.

The Hammers made a second trip north of the border on Saturday 24 July when David Moyes' side ran in six goals in a pre-season goal fest at Celtic, defeating the Scottish Premiership side 6-2.

The visitors scored three in each half, coming from 1-0 down to lead 3-1 at the break thanks to Michail Antonio's double and a Mark Noble penalty. Said Benrahma, Jarrod Bowen and Armstrong Okoflex got in on the act after the restart to round off a highly entertaining 90 minutes in Glasgow.

With 18,000 fans permitted back in Celtic Park for the first time since the covid-19 pandemic broke out, this game really gave both sides a feeling of normality and added some reality to their pre-season preparations.

Benrahma then netted a sublime goal on his return to Brentford to give West Ham United a fourth straight pre-season win when they took on Premier League new boys Brentford on Saturday 31 July.

Benrahma spent two years with the Bees, prior to heading across London to the Hammers, and he reminded the west Londoners of his abilities with a beautiful, curling strike which gave his team a 1-0 win on their first trip to Brentford's Community Stadium.

DECLAN RICE SHOOTS FOR GOAL V ATALANTA

LANZINI V BRENTFORD

ANTONIO CELEBRATES HIS GOAL AGAINST ATALANTA

West Ham United clinched an unbeaten pre-season campaign - and their first Betway Cup victory since 2018 - with a professional 2-0 win over Serie A heavyweights Atalanta at London Stadium on Saturday 7 August.

The Hammers put in a promising display ahead of their Premier League opener against the Magpies as goals at the tail end of both halves - both set up by Said Benrahma - clinched victory.

A high-tempo match yielded plenty of entertainment for a buoyant home support, with the win set on its way when Benrahma capitalised on a miscommunication at the back to chip the ball over the top for Michail Antonio, who thrashed home seconds prior to half-time.

West Ham had been the better side during the opening period and continued to carve out opportunities in the second, capped off when Benrahma's stooping header from Ryan Fredericks' cross was deflected into the net by Pablo Fornals.

MANUEL LANZINI

GOAL
OF THE
SEASON

16

PABLO FORNALS
V LEICESTER CITY (H), 4 OCTOBER 2020

MANUEL LANZINI
V TOTTENHAM HOTSPUR (A), 18 OCTOBER 2020

MICHAIL ANTONIO
V MANCHESTER CITY (H), 24 OCTOBER 2020

SEBASTIEN HALLER
V CRYSTAL PALACE (H), 16 DECEMBER 2020

TOMAS SOUCEK
V ASTON VILLA (A), 3 FEBRUARY 2021

JESSE LINGARD
V TOTTENHAM HOTSPUR (H), 21 FEBRUARY 2021

JESSE LINGARD
V ARSENAL (H), 21 MARCH 2021

JESSE LINGARD
V WOLVERHAMPTON WANDERERS (H), 5 APRIL 2021

PABLO FORNALS
V WOLVERHAMPTON WANDERERS (A), 5 APRIL 2021

SAID BENRAHMA
V BRIGHTON & HOVE ALBION (A), 15 MAY 2021

The 2020/21 season saw West Ham United score an impressive 76 goals in all competitions and that goal total ensured the Hammers progressed in both domestic cup competitions while ending their Premier League campaign in sixth place.

The team's 62 Premier League goals that landed David Moyes' men a top-six finish also secured qualification for the group stages of the 2021/22 Europa League. In what was a memorable and successful season, but dampened by the covid-19 pandemic resulting in most matches played in empty stadiums, there were a host of great goals for Hammers' fans to choose from when it came to voting for the club's prestigious Goal of the Season accolade.

Everyone will have their favourite goal and for all manner of different reasons, but when it came to casting a vote for the Goal of the Season award, there was a pre-selected top ten to choose from. Despite the competition almost becoming the Jesse Lingard show in the second-half of the season, there could only be one winner and a clear favourite soon emerged.

The winner was Manuel Lanzini's brilliant long-range strike in injury time that rescued a point in an astonishing comeback away to Spurs on Sunday 18 October 2020.

3-0 down at London-rivals Spurs with eight minutes left to play, West Ham looked dead and buried. But Fabian Balbuena's header and a Davinson Sanchez own goal gave the visitors hope. It was hope that Manuel Lanzini cashed in on with a quite magnificent leveller in the fourth minute of stoppage time.

Aaron Cresswell's wide free-kick was headed out to Lanzini, who paid no attention to Harry Winks closing in, fading an unstoppable first-time 25-yard shot beyond Hugo Lloris' reach and into the top corner. What a moment!

Lanzini's goal really had the lot - imagination, technique, perfect execution and all in the most dramatic of circumstances.

The only ingredient missing from such a magical moment was of course, the claret and blue army who would have ensured the visitors' section at the Tottenham Hotspur Stadium was a sea of euphoria, had supporters been in attendance. If ever there was a game and a goal that warranted a full stadium then surely this was it.

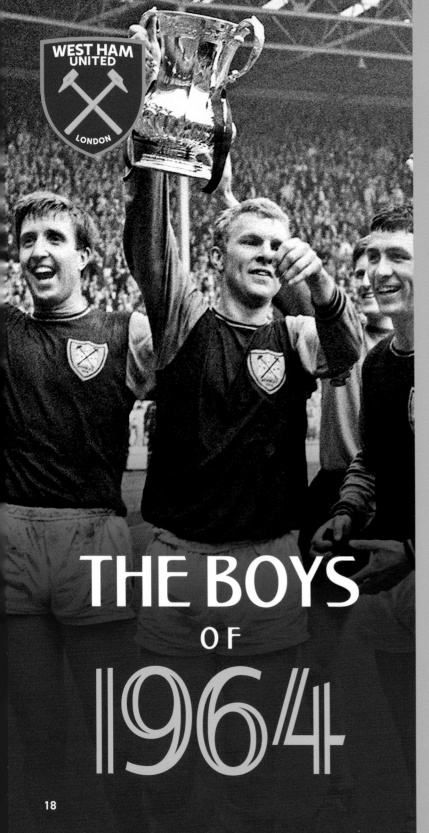

THE BOYS OF 1964

Under the management of Ron Greenwood, West Ham United secured a 14th-place First Division finish in 1963/64, but once again, it was the FA Cup that provided a real buzz around the Boleyn Ground.

Having bowed out of the competition at the quarter-final stage the previous season, West Ham had developed a real quest for cup glory and in 1963/64 they reached the Wembley final for the first time since 1923.

This historic cup run began with a 3-0 London derby victory over Charlton Athletic. Defeating the Addicks handed the Hammers another London opponent in the fourth round when they were paired with near-neighbours Leyton Orient. A 1-1 draw at Brisbane Road was followed by 3-0 victory in the Boleyn replay as Greenwood's men landed the reward of a fifth-round trip to Swindon Town.

A 3-1 win over the Robins saw the Hammers face an all First Division tie at home to Burnley in the quarter-final. The Clarets clash was a pulsating affair for the 36,651 sell-out crowd as a Johnny Byrne brace and a goal from teenage winger John Sissons saw the Hammers edge a five-goal thriller 3-2.

Title-chasing Manchester United provided West Ham United's semi-final opposition on 14 March 1964 at Hillsborough. Two goals early in the second half from Ronnie Boyce put the Hammers in the driving seat and within touching distance of Wembley.

However, the tie was put right back into the melting pot when Denis Law reduced the arrears after 77 minutes. Concern didn't last too long for the Hammers' fans though as Geoff Hurst established the Irons' two-goal cushion just two minutes later and that proved enough to take West Ham to Wembley.

Second Division Preston North End now stood between West Ham United and a first major trophy. Despite the Hammers stepping out at Wembley as firm favourites, it was North End who engineered a tenth-minute opening goal. West Ham were soon back in the game, Sissons levelling only a minute later.

Still, West Ham had it all to do in the second half after falling 2-1 down five minutes before the break. Seven minutes into the second period and it was 2-2 thanks to a header from Hurst.

As the match entered its final minute, and extra time beckoning, Peter Bradbrook sent in a cross from the right and Boyce arrived right on cue to head home the winner and spark scenes delight for all of a Claret and Blue persuasion.

STAR MAN

RONNIE BOYCE

A one-club man, midfielder Ronnie Boyce enjoyed a 341-game West Ham United playing career with the 1963/64 FA Cup triumph being arguably his finest hour.

One of the first names on Ron Greenwood's teamsheet, Boyce's two goals against Manchester United in the Hillsborough semi-final and then his dramatic last-gasp winner at Wembley have seen his name etched into West Ham United folklore.

Boyce was also a member of the Hammers side that won the European Cup Winners' Cup the following season, but his name will always remain associated with the club's FA Cup success of 1964 above all else.

BOBBY MOORE

RONNIE BOYCE'S LAST-MINUTE WINNER

JOHN SISSONS & GEOFF HURST

19

ANSWERS ON PAGE 82

THE SQUAD
2021 22

2021 22

LUKASZ FABIANSKI

POSITION: Goalkeeper **DoB:** 18/04/1985 **BIRTHPLACE:** Kostrzyn nad Odra, Poland

The 2020/21 season was another successful campaign for Lukasz Fabianski. The Poland international goalkeeper, who joined West Ham United in the summer of 2018 from Swansea City, started 35 of the Hammers' 38 Premier League matches, keeping ten clean sheets in the process. He was then named in Poland's squad for the delayed UEFA Euro 2020 - his fifth major tournament for his country.

The 6' 3" stopper was quick to make his mark at the London Stadium and was named Hammer of the Year after his debut campaign with the Club in 2018/19, which saw him feature in all 38 Premier League matches. A hip injury in September 2019 saw him miss part of the 2019/20 campaign, but he still played in 26 matches overall while he made 37 appearances in all competitions in 2020/21.

Prior to West Ham United, the Pole represented Lech Poznan, Legia Warsaw - for whom he won the Ekstraklasa title in 2005/06 - and Arsenal, where he was an FA Cup winner in 2014, before his move to Swansea City in 2014.

3

AARON CRESSWELL

POSITION: Defender **DoB:** 15/12/1989 **BIRTHPLACE:** Liverpool

Now in his eighth season with West Ham United, Aaron Cresswell continues to be of the Club's most consistent performers.

The Liverpool-born left-back, who began his career with Tranmere Rovers, made eight assists in 36 Premier League matches in 2020/21 - more than any other defender in the division. Cresswell joined West Ham United from Ipswich Town in the summer of 2014 on the back of being named in the PFA's Championship Team of the Year. He won the Hammer of the Year award at the end of his debut season with the Club in 2014/15 and has since gone on to make over 250 appearances for the Irons.

Amongst his most memorable moments in a Hammers shirt was his stunning free-kick in a 2-0 win over Manchester United at London Stadium in September 2019 and his winning goal in a 1-0 Premier triumph at Chelsea two months later.

A reliable full-back who is rarely beaten in one-on-one situations, Cresswell has been capped three times by England and remains contracted to West Ham United until 2023.

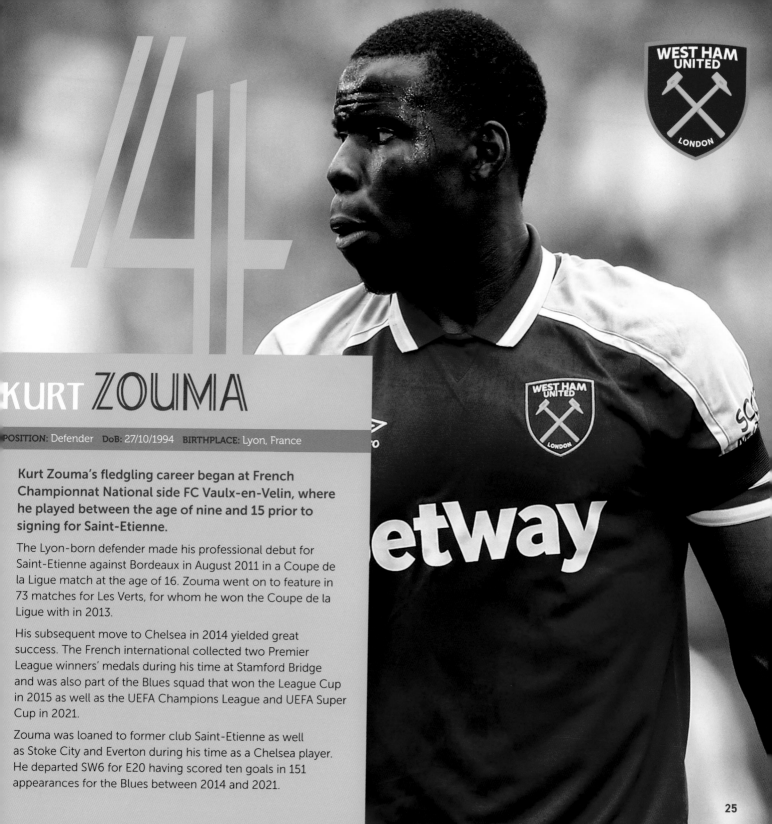

KURT ZOUMA

4

POSITION: Defender **DoB:** 27/10/1994 **BIRTHPLACE:** Lyon, France

Kurt Zouma's fledgling career began at French Championnat National side FC Vaulx-en-Velin, where he played between the age of nine and 15 prior to signing for Saint-Etienne.

The Lyon-born defender made his professional debut for Saint-Etienne against Bordeaux in August 2011 in a Coupe de la Ligue match at the age of 16. Zouma went on to feature in 73 matches for Les Verts, for whom he won the Coupe de la Ligue with in 2013.

His subsequent move to Chelsea in 2014 yielded great success. The French international collected two Premier League winners' medals during his time at Stamford Bridge and was also part of the Blues squad that won the League Cup in 2015 as well as the UEFA Champions League and UEFA Super Cup in 2021.

Zouma was loaned to former club Saint-Etienne as well as Stoke City and Everton during his time as a Chelsea player. He departed SW6 for E20 having scored ten goals in 151 appearances for the Blues between 2014 and 2021.

VLADIMIR COUFAL

POSITION: Defender **DoB:** 22/08/1992 **BIRTHPLACE:** Ostrava, Czechoslovakia

Vladimir Coufal was named runner-up in the 2021 Hammer of the Year award and picked up the Signing of the Season accolade after a fantastic debut campaign with West Ham United. The Czech Republic international right-back made a total 32 Premier League and two FA Cup appearances during the season.

Having arrived from Slavia Prague on a three-year deal in October 2020, Coufal made his debut in a 3-0 Premier League win at Leicester City that same month. He made seven assists during the campaign - the second highest tally for a defender anywhere in the league. Only teammate Aaron Cresswell with eight managed more assists in 2020/21, meaning the pair were head and shoulders above any other Premier League full-back duo in terms of the number of goals they created.

Coufal was included in the Czech Republic's squad for the delayed UEFA Euro 2020 tournament, where he made five appearances.

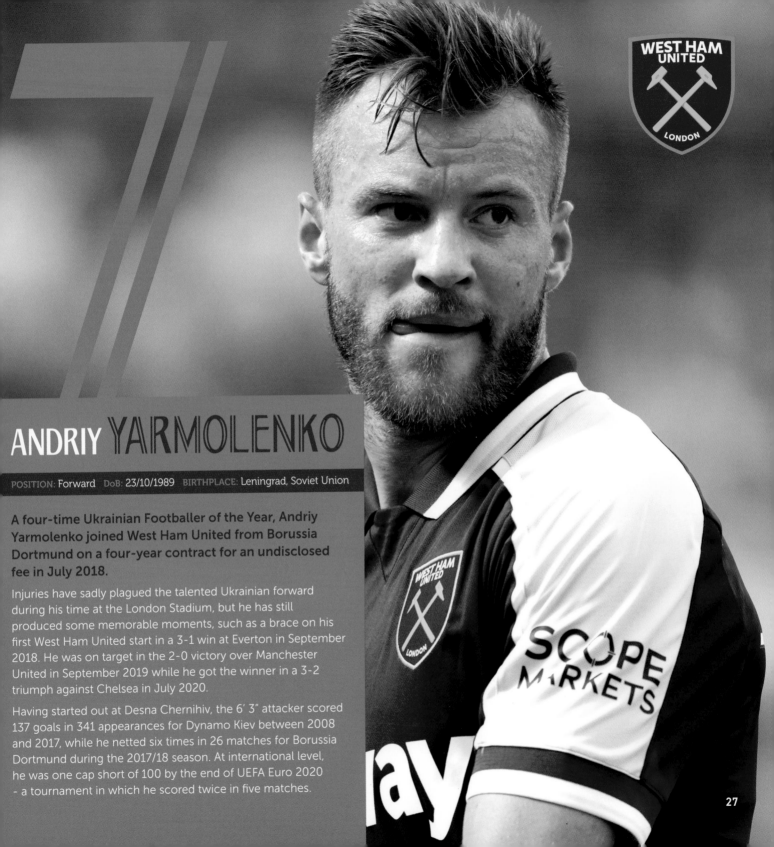

ANDRIY YARMOLENKO

POSITION: Forward   **DoB:** 23/10/1989   **BIRTHPLACE:** Leningrad, Soviet Union

A four-time Ukrainian Footballer of the Year, Andriy Yarmolenko joined West Ham United from Borussia Dortmund on a four-year contract for an undisclosed fee in July 2018.

Injuries have sadly plagued the talented Ukrainian forward during his time at the London Stadium, but he has still produced some memorable moments, such as a brace on his first West Ham United start in a 3-1 win at Everton in September 2018. He was on target in the 2-0 victory over Manchester United in September 2019 while he got the winner in a 3-2 triumph against Chelsea in July 2020.

Having started out at Desna Chernihiv, the 6' 3" attacker scored 137 goals in 341 appearances for Dynamo Kiev between 2008 and 2017, while he netted six times in 26 matches for Borussia Dortmund during the 2017/18 season. At international level, he was one cap short of 100 by the end of UEFA Euro 2020 - a tournament in which he scored twice in five matches.

PABLO FORNALS

POSITION: Midfielder **DoB:** 22/02/1996 **BIRTHPLACE:** Castellon, Spain

Spanish international Pablo Fornals has been a near ever-present for West Ham United since signing from Villarreal in June 2019 on a five-year contract.

The technically-gifted playmaker started his career at Malaga, for whom he scored seven goals in 63 appearances. His two seasons at Villarreal in 2017/18 and 2018/19 saw him score nine goals in 96 matches meanwhile. His senior Spain debut came against Switzerland in May 2016.

Fornals made his competitive Hammers debut against Manchester City in August 2019, while he first goal for the Club followed in a 2-0 EFL Cup victory at Newport County later that month. He scored three times in 39 appearances in his debut season for West Ham United in 2019/20, while he netted six times in 36 matches the following campaign.

Fornals started the 2021/22 season in impressive fashion, scoring in the 4-1 win over Leicester City and the 2-2 draw with Crystal Palace at London Stadium in August 2021.

MICHAIL ANTONIO

POSITION: Forward   **DoB:** 28/03/1990   **BIRTHPLACE:** Wandsworth

A firm favourite amongst the West Ham United faithful, Michael Antonio joined the Hammers from Nottingham Forest in September 2015.

The Wandsworth-born forward enjoyed an impressive first season in claret and blue, with nine goals in 32 matches in 2015/16. He followed that up with nine goals in 37 games in 2016/17 as he landed the coveted Hammer of the Year award and put pen-to-paper on a new four-year contract.

Fast-forwarding to the 2019/20 season, Antonio was West Ham United's top goal scorer with ten strikes in 26 matches. He was joint-top scorer in 2020/21, as he matched his goals and appearance record of the previous campaign.

He started the 2021/22 season in impressive form, with a strike in the 4-2 away victory at Newcastle United and a brace in the 4-1 home win over Leicester City in August 2021. His opener against the Foxes saw him become the Irons top, all-time goal scorer in the Premier League with 48 strikes.

THE SQUAD
2021
22

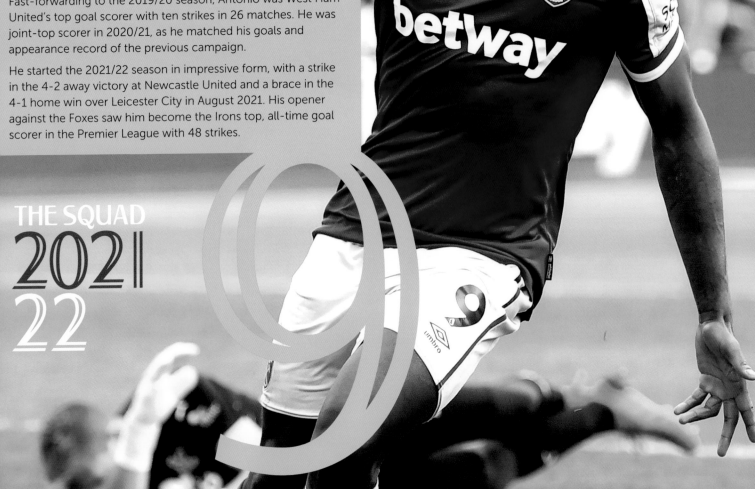

29

10

MANUEL LANZINI

POSITION: Midfielder   **DoB:** 15/02/1993   **BIRTHPLACE:** Ituzaingo, Argentina

Attacking midfielder Manuel Lanzini is an exciting Argentina international who has got West Ham United fans off their seats regularly since joining the club in the summer of 2015.

A naturally gifted playmaker, Lanzini learned his trade at River Plate in his native Buenos Aires, where he won the Torneo Final title in 2014 - two years after winning the Campeonato Carioca and Brasileiro Serie A during a season on loan with Brazilian side Fluminense.

Lanzini moved to the UAE Arabian Gulf League with Al Jazira Club in 2014, where he again excelled before being loaned to the Hammers. Following a highly-impressive first season with the Irons, he completed a permanent move to West ham United ahead of the 2016/17 campaign.

After playing his 100th Premier League match for West Ham in August 2019, Lanzini agreed a new long-term contract with the club. Despite sustaining a dislocated shoulder in an away game at Burnley in November 2019, he was still able to make 26 appearances during the 2019/20 season, while he netted once in 23 matches for the Hammers in 2020/21.

THE SQUAD
2021
22

NIKOLA VLASIC

POSITION: Midfielder DoB: 04/10/1997 BIRTHPLACE: Split, Croatia

After a series of impressive showings at the delayed UEFA Euro 2020 - a tournament in which he scored once in four appearances for Croatia - Nikola Vlasic signed for West Ham United from CSKA Moscow in August 2021.

The attacking midfielder started his senior club career at Hajduk Split, for whom he scored on his debut against Dundalk in a UEFA Europa League match in July 2014, aged just 16 at the time. He went on to score 13 goals in 120 appearances for Split prior to a transfer to Everton in August 2017.

Vlasic was loaned to CSKA Moscow during the 2018/19 season - a move that was made permanent in June 2019. He departed Goodison Park having scored two goals in 19 appearances in all competitions.

The Croatian international was a big hit in the Russian capital, scoring eight goals and making seven assists in his debut season with CSKA in 2018/19 - which he followed up with 13 strikes and seven assists in 2019/20.

The 2020/21 season saw Vlasic named Russian Premier League, Russian Football Union and Sport Express Footballer of the Year.

13

ALPHONSE AREOLA

POSITION: Goalkeeper **DoB:** 27/02/1993 **BIRTHPLACE:** Paris, France

FIFA World Cup-winning goalkeeper Alphonse Areola joined West Ham United on an initial season-long loan from Paris Saint-Germain in July 2021, with the option to make the transfer permanent in the summer of 2022.

Areola rose through the ranks at PSG to made his first-team debut in May 2013 at the age of 20. He has since gone on to make 107 appearances for the French giants, for whom he won the Ligue 1 title on three occasions.

The French goalkeeper has been loaned to a number of different clubs during his career, the first such deal took him to RC Lens in 2013/14. He spent the 2014/15 season with Bastia and the 2015/16 campaign with Villarreal.

In September 2019, Areola joined Real Madrid on a season-long loan as part of the deal which saw Keylor Navas sign for PSG. The 6' 5" stopper made nine appearances in all competitions for Los Blancos, who won the La Liga in title in 2019/20. He was named Fulham's Player of the Season meanwhile as the result of another successful loan in 2020/21.

15

CRAIG DAWSON

POSITION: Defender **DoB:** 06/05/1990 **BIRTHPLACE:** Rochdale

Former Rochdale, West Bromwich Albion and Bolton Wanderers defender Craig Dawson joined West Ham United on loan from Watford in October 2020. He made his Hammers debut against Southampton in December 2020 and was named Man of the Match for his performance in the goalless draw at St Mary's Stadium.

Dawson's first Irons goal proved to be the winner in the 1-0 triumph at Stockport County in FA Cup third round in January 2021. He scored two more goals that month - one in the 3-2 Premier League win at Crystal Palace and another in the 3-1 home defeat by Liverpool.

Dawson's fourth goal of the season came in the 2-0 win over Leeds United at London Stadium in March 2021. The following month, it was announced that the defender would be joining the Hammers on a permanent basis at the end of the 2020/21 campaign, as he signed a two-year contract. The defender ended his debut season at West Ham United having made a total of 24 appearances for the Club in all competitions.

16

MARK NOBLE

POSITION: Midfielder **DoB:** 08/05/1987 **BIRTHPLACE:** Canning Town

Very much the modern day 'Mr West Ham United', Mark Noble has been synonymous with the Irons since he made his debut for the club as a 17-year-old in August 2004.

Since then, the Canning Town-born midfielder has won two Hammer of the Year awards, twice won promotion to the Premier League and amassed more than 500 first-team appearances in Claret and Blue - one of only ten players to reach that landmark. In December 2017, he became the first West Ham player to make 300 Premier League appearances while his 500th appearance for the Club came against Watford in July 2020.

Noble's commitment to the cause saw him rewarded with a Testimonial in 2016 - the same year he captained the Hammers in their final game at the Boleyn Ground and first match at London Stadium.

In March 2021, Noble put pen-to-paper on a new one-year contract with the Club, announcing at the same time the 2021/22 campaign will be his last with West Ham United.

**THE SQUAD
2021
22**

20

JARROD BOWEN

POSITION: Forward   **DoB:** 20/12/1996   **BIRTHPLACE:** Leominster

A prolific goalscorer who has the versatility to operate almost anywhere across the front line, Jarrod Bowen joined West Ham United from Hull City on the final day of the 2020 January transfer window.

After joining the Tigers from non-league Hereford United in the summer of 2014, Bowen proved to be a constant thorn in the side of defenders at both Premier League and Championship level. Blessed with natural speed and a hard-working approach, Bowen was widely considered as one of the best players in the Championship prior to his arrival at London Stadium in January 2020.

Following his multi-million pound move, Bowen debuted for the Hammers away to Manchester City before marking his first start with a goal in the 3-1 home win over Southampton in February 2020.

Having made 13 appearances for the Club in 2019/20, Bowen established himself as a first-team regular in 2020/21. He featured in all 38 Premier League matches and scored eight goals, including three strikes in as many games in a 3-3 draw with Arsenal and 3-2 victories over Wolverhampton Wanderers and Leicester City.

21

ANGELO OGBONNA

POSITION: Defender   **DoB:** 23/05/1988   **BIRTHPLACE:** Cassino, Italy

Angelo Ogbonna signed for West Ham United from Italian champions Juventus in summer 2015.

The strong and powerful central-defender, who can also play at left-back, started his career with Torino before moving across the city and winning back-to-back Serie A titles in 2014 and 2015.

A UEFA Euro 2012 runner-up and Euro 2016 squad member, Ogbonna enjoyed a memorable debut campaign with West Ham and etched his name into Hammers' folklore with an unforgettable extra-time FA Cup winner against Liverpool at the Boleyn Ground in February 2016.

After debuting in the Hammers' 2-0 London derby success away to Arsenal on the opening day of the 2015/16 season, Ogbonna has amassed almost 200 appearances in Claret and Blue. He featured in 29 matches in all competitions for West Ham in 2020/21, scoring three times. That included the winning goal in a 2-1 away triumph at Leeds United in the Irons' first win at Elland Road since 2000.

THE SQUAD
2021
22

SAID BENRAHMA

POSITION: Forward **DoB:** 10/08/1995 **BIRTHPLACE:** Aïn Témouchent, Algeria

Having previously represented the likes of Nice, Anger, Ajaccio and Chateauroux in France, Said Benrahma joined Brentford back in 2018. The attack-minded player made a real impression in west London, scoring 30 goals and making 27 assists in 94 appearances for the Bees.

He picked up a number of individual accolades along with way, including the Bees Supporters' Player of the Year award in 2020, while he was also named in the Championship PFA Team of the Year in 2019/20.

Benrahma joined West Ham United on a season-long loan in October 2020, making his debut for the Club against Liverpool later that month. His first start came against Leeds United in December 2020. The Algerian international's transfer to West Ham was made permanent in January 2021.

Benrahma's first Hammers goal came in a 1-1 draw at Brighton & Hove Albion in May 2021 while he netted in the first two matches of the 2021/22 season, in a 4-2 win at Newcastle United and a 4-1 home triumph over Leicester City in the Premier League.

ISSA DIOP

POSITION: Defender **DoB:** 09/01/1997 **BIRTHPLACE:** Toulouse, France

West Ham United signed Issa Diop for a then-club record transfer fee from Ligue 1 club Toulouse back in June 2018.

The talented centre-back signed a five-year contract and made his club debut away to Arsenal in August 2018. He scored his first Hammers goal in a EFL Cup game against Wimbledon days later, while his performance in the 3-1 win over Manchester United drew praise from ex-Reds boss Jose Mourinho.

A model of consistency, Diop had made 95 West Ham United appearances and scored seven goals by the end of his third season with the Club in 2020/21. The aforementioned campaign saw him net twice in 21 matches, with goals in the 3-0 home win over Sheffield United in February 2021 and the 3-2 defeat at Newcastle United in April 2021.

At international level, Diop has been capped at every age-group level from under-16 to under-21. He won the UEFA European under-19 Championship with France in 2016, scoring his country's fourth goal in a 4-0 victory over Italy in the final.

RYAN FREDERICKS

POSITION: Defender **DoB:** 10/10/1992 **BIRTHPLACE:** Hammersmith

Ryan Fredericks was former West Ham United manager Manuel Pellegrini's first signing as Hammers boss back in July 2018. The defender has been a consistent performer ever since, with 62 Hammers appearances and three goals to his name prior to the start of the 2021/22 season.

Ex-Tottenham Hotspur, Brentford (loan), Millwall (loan), Middlesbrough (loan) and Bristol City man Fredericks excelled at another of his former clubs, Fulham. He arrived at London Stadium on the back of the 2017/18 campaign, that saw him named in the PFA Championship Team of the Year as the Whites won promotion to the Premier League.

Blessed with blistering pace, Fredericks can fill either the right-back and right wing-back position with equal competence. He also deputised as a right-sided midfield during the 2020/21 season, producing an excellent performance in that position in a 3-1 win at Aston Villa in February 2021, while he scored in a 3-0 home win over Sheffield United that same month. Fredericks made a total of 16 appearances in all competitions during the 2020/21 campaign, with six starts and eight substitute appearances in the Premier League.

DAVID MARTIN

POSITION: Goalkeeper **DoB:** 22/01/1986 **BIRTHPLACE:** Romford

The son of a West Ham United legend - FA Cup winner and former skipper, Alvin Martin - David Martin was born in Romford and grew up a supporter of the Irons, spending his summers with his father at the club's Chadwell Heath training ground.

David trained with Tottenham Hotspur, West Ham United and Wimbledon as a youngster, starting his senior career at the latter. After spells with the likes of Liverpool, Accrington Stanley (loan), Leicester City (loan), Tranmere Rovers (loan), Leeds United (loan) and Derby County (loan), the goalkeeper signed for Millwall in 2017.

He moved to his boyhood club on a free transfer in July 2019 with his Hammers' debut coming a memorable 1-0 away win at Chelsea in November 2019 which saw him presented with the man of the match award. He made five appearances during the 2019/20 season, but wasn't called upon in 2020/21.

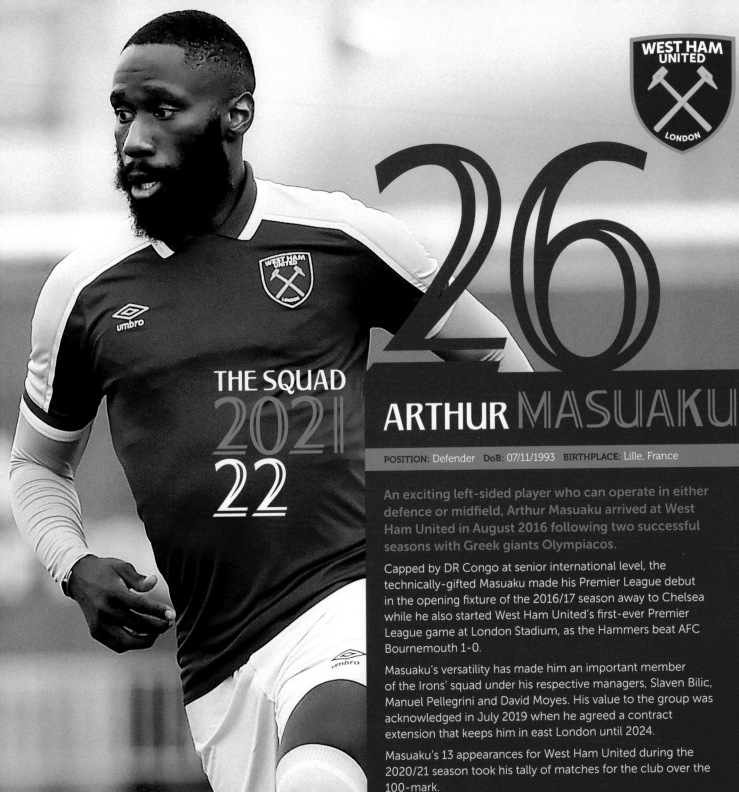

26

ARTHUR MASUAKU

POSITION: Defender   **DoB:** 07/11/1993   **BIRTHPLACE:** Lille, France

THE SQUAD
2021
22

An exciting left-sided player who can operate in either defence or midfield, Arthur Masuaku arrived at West Ham United in August 2016 following two successful seasons with Greek giants Olympiacos.

Capped by DR Congo at senior international level, the technically-gifted Masuaku made his Premier League debut in the opening fixture of the 2016/17 season away to Chelsea while he also started West Ham United's first-ever Premier League game at London Stadium, as the Hammers beat AFC Bournemouth 1-0.

Masuaku's versatility has made him an important member of the Irons' squad under his respective managers, Slaven Bilic, Manuel Pellegrini and David Moyes. His value to the group was acknowledged in July 2019 when he agreed a contract extension that keeps him in east London until 2024.

Masuaku's 13 appearances for West Ham United during the 2020/21 season took his tally of matches for the club over the 100-mark.

28

TOMAS SOUCEK

POSITION: Midfielder **DoB:** 27/02/1995 **BIRTHPLACE:** Havlickuv Brod, Czech Republic

Tomas Soucek was named as the 2021 Hammer of the Year on the back of a season in which he was a Premier League ever-present for West Ham United - starting and finishing all 38 league matches.

The Czech Republic international midfielder finished the 2020/21 campaign as the Club's joint-leading scorer too, tied on ten goals with Michail Antonio.

Soucek originally arrived at West Ham United on loan from Slavia Prague in January 2020. His transfer was made permanent in July 2020, when he agreed a four-year deal at London Stadium. Prior to that, the towering central-midfielder won two Czech First League titles and two Czech Cups during an outstanding career in his homeland that also saw him excel in the UEFA Champions League and UEFA Europa League for Slavia.

Soucek is a true energetic box-to-box midfielder who boasts exceptional defensive and attacking qualities. He netted his first Hammers' goal in a 3-2 victory over Chelsea in July 2020.

BEN JOHNSON

POSITION: Defender **DoB:** 22/01/2000 **BIRTHPLACE:** Waltham Forest

Having originally joined West Ham United at the age of seven, Ben Johnson has risen through the ranks to establish himself in the Hammers first-team.

The defender was named the 2020/21 Young Hammer of the Year, on the back of a season in which he made 20 senior appearances. He scored his first goal for the Club in a 2-2 draw with Brighton & Hove Albion in December 2020.

The attack-minded full-back, who is able to operate on both sides of the pitch, was first named in the Hammers' senior squad for a 2-1 defeat at Manchester City in December 2017, when he was an unused substitute. His debut followed in February 2019, as he started a Premier League match, also away to Manchester City, at left-back.

Johnson, who is the nephew of former England full-back Paul Parker and the cousin of ex-Tottenham Hotspur captain Ledley King, signed his first professional contract in December 2017 and put pen-to-paper on a new, three-year deal in March 2019.

ALEX KRAL

POSITION: Midfielder **DoB:** 19/05/1998 **BIRTHPLACE:** Kosice, Slovakia

Czech Republic international Alex Kral joined West Ham United on a season-long loan from Spartak Moscow on transfer deadline day in August 2021.

Kral featured in four of the Czech Republic's five matches at the delayed UEFA Euro 2020, which saw them reach the quarter-finals. The defensive midfielder has won over 20 caps for his country, since making his senior international debut against Brazil in a friendly in March 2019. He previously represented his country at all levels between U17 and U21.

Club-wise, Kral started his professional career with Czech First League club Teplice prior to a move to Slavia Prague in January 2019, for whom he went on to score once in 29 appearances. His displays for Slavia brought him to the attention of Russian Premier League side Spartak Moscow, who signed him on a five-year deal in September 2019.

Kral is part of the same West Ham United squad as fellow Czech internationals Vladimir Coufal and Tomas Soucek.

41

35

DARREN RANDOLPH

POSITION: Goalkeeper   **DoB:** 12/05/1987   **BIRTHPLACE:** Bray, Republic of Ireland

Republic of Ireland international goalkeeper Darren Randolph began his second spell with West Ham United in January 2020 when he rejoined the club from Middlesbrough during the transfer window.

The 34-year-old stopper began his career with Charlton Athletic and initially joined the Hammers from Birmingham City as a free agent in the summer of 2015. Having played in the club's final game at the Boleyn Ground and also the first competitive fixture at London Stadium, Randolph has already etched his name in to West Ham history.

Blessed with lightning-fast reactions and an ability to organise those in front of him, Randolph established himself as the Hammers' first choice 'keeper in 2016/17, but opted to join Middlesbrough following Joe Hart's arrival at West Ham.

Randolph made over a century of league appearances for Boro, but with new manager David Moyes keen to bolster his goalkeeping options, Randolph jumped at the chance of a return to the Premier League and West Ham United. He featured in three competitive matches during the 2019/20 season and seven in 2020/21.

42

41

DECLAN RICE

POSITION: Midfielder **DoB:** 14/01/1999 **BIRTHPLACE:** Kingston upon Thames

Declan Rice was a standout performer for England at the delayed UEFA Euro 2020 - a tournament in which he appeared in all seven of the Three Lions' matches including the final. This followed on from an excellent club season, in which he scored twice in 35 games in all competitions for the Hammers.

Rice, who won the prestigious Hammer of the Year accolade in 2019/20, first joined the club at the age of 14. He captained the Hammers at under-16, under-18 and under-23 level before making his first-team debut in a Premier League win at Burnley in the final game of the 2016/17 season. A year later, at 19, he finished as runner-up in the Hammer of the Year voting.

Having previously represented the Republic of Ireland between under-16 and senior level, Rice switched his international allegiance to England in 2019 and made his Three Lions debut against the Czech Republic at Wembley Stadium in March 2019.

Comfortable playing at centre-back or as a defensive midfielder, Rice was just five senior appearances off 150 matches at the start of the 2021/22 season.

ROBERT SNODGRASS OPENS THE SPRING V HULL CITY IN AN EMPTY LONDON STADIUM

YARMOLENKO SCORES FROM THE SPOT V HULL CITY

JARROD BOWEN NET THE FIRST OF HIS BRACE V WOLVES

2020/21

REVIEW

Celebrating the club's first 125 years throughout 2020/21, West Ham United had to tackle their 126th season without the backing of their loyal and passionate supporters for the majority of the 2020/21 campaign.

With the ongoing covid-19 pandemic resulting in matches being played behind closed doors, David Moyes' men, and the rest of football, faced up to the challenge of silent, soulless stadiums and competing in an environment that was drastically removed from the game we all know and love.

However, the Hammers managed the strange circumstances superbly and ended an excellent season with a club record 65 Premier League points and with it, a sixth-place finish. That achievement resulted in qualification for the Europa League in 2021/22 - something supporters will no doubt relish as they return to stadiums for the new season.

Following the late conclusion of the previous season, via the summer's project re-start fixtures, the 2020/21 Premier League campaign did not begin until mid-September. Suffice to say, when the Hammers opened with a 2-0 defeat at home to Newcastle United, few saw European qualification on the agenda. A comprehensive League Cup victory over Charlton Athletic was followed by a trip to Arsenal where Michail Antonio's first goal of the season looked to have won the Hammers their first point of the campaign, only for a late strike from Eddie Nketiah to seal a 2-1 win for the Gunners.

Although early Premier League points were proving tough to come by, League Cup progress continued with a 5-1 thrashing of League One Hull City at London Stadium. It proved to be a case of third time luck in the Premier League as a Jarrod Bowen brace helped inspire a comprehensive 4-0 home win over Wolves.

The opening month of the season may have ended with a League Cup exit at Everton, but the month of October began in style as the Hammers produced a thoroughly professional performance to win 3-0 away to Leicester City. Next up was a London derby at Spurs which with eight minutes remaining appeared to be heading for disaster. Trailing 3-0, the visitors mounted a sensational late comeback and secured a most unlikely point when Manuel Lanzini netted an unforgettable 94th-minute equaliser.

LANZINI IS MOBBED BY TEAMMATES AT TOTTENHAM HOTSPUR STADIUM

BOWEN CELEBRATES SCORING THE THIRD AT LEICESTER

SOUCEK SCORES AGAINST THE RED DEVILS IN FRONT ON 2000 FANS AT LONDON

October continued with Antonio on the mark as West Ham then took a point from their home game against Manchester City before surrendering an early lead to lose 2-1 at champions Liverpool.

Tomas Soucek's first goal of the season saw the Irons start November with a London-derby triumph over Fulham. That win was the first of three back-to-back Premier League victories as the month concluded with a 1-0 win at Sheffield United and a 2-1 victory at home to Aston Villa.

The hectic month of December kicked off with a 3-1 defeat to Manchester United at London Stadium and saw a brief return of fans to the stadium with 2,000 taking part in a limited capacity test event. Despite that loss, Moyes' men bounced back in style as they came from behind to win 2-1 at newly-promoted Leeds United on 11 December.

Two London derbies followed, a point was gained at home to Crystal Palace before the Hammers suffered a disappointing pre-Christmas defeat to Chelsea at Stamford Bridge. Two second-half equalisers were needed to earn a point at home to Brighton on 27 December before the calendar year of 2020 ended with goalless draw at Southampton.

West Ham enjoyed an exceptional start to 2021 as they reeled off six straight wins - four of which came in the Premier League, while also enjoying FA Cup progression at the expense of Stockport County (1-0 away) and Doncaster Rovers (4-0 at home). The year began with a late Soucek goal on New Year's Day that gave manager Moyes a triumphant return to Goodison Park as Everton were beaten 1-0. Antonio then netted the only goal of the game to secure a hard-fought victory over Burnley at London Stadium and the ace marksman was at it again three days later as he grabbed the winner in a 2-1 home win over struggling West Bromwich Albion.

Next up was a thrilling five-goal London derby with Crysta Palace at Selhurst Park which saw Soucek as the Hammers two-goal hero in a 3-2 success. The only blemish on the month was a 3-1 home defeat to reigning champions Liverpool on 31 January. Despite the Liverpool defeat, the month ended on a positive note with the signing of attacking midfielder Jesse Lingard who joined on loan for the remainder of the season from Manchester United.

Lingard marked his Hammers' debut with a brace in the 3-1 win away to Aston Villa on 3 February and the team then displayed all their battling qualities to leave Craven Cottage with a point following a goalless draw with Fulham.

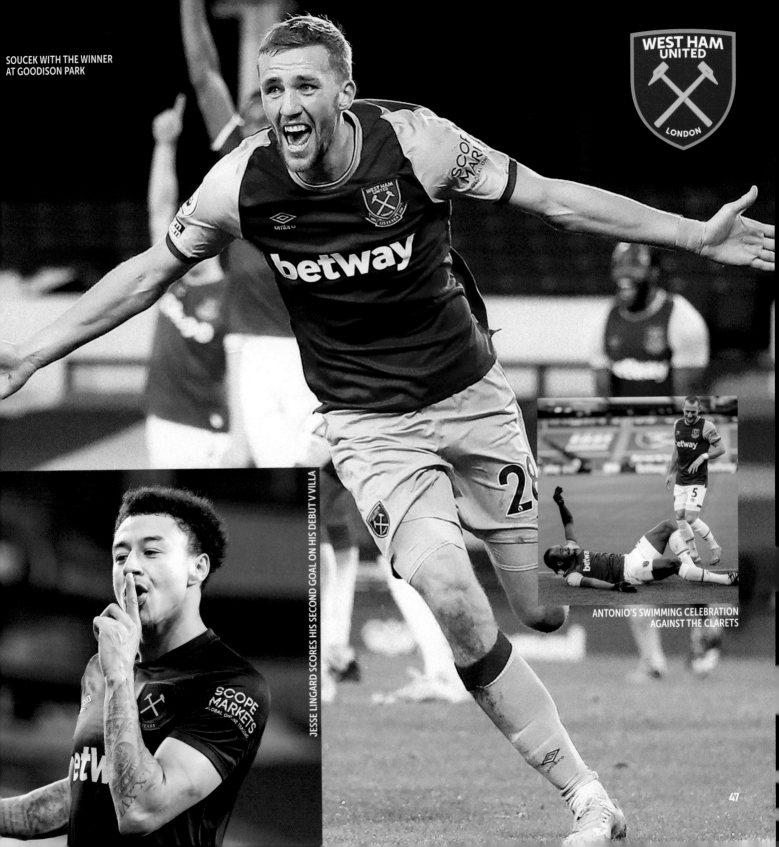

SOUCEK WITH THE WINNER AT GOODISON PARK

WEST HAM UNITED LONDON

JESSE LINGARD SCORES HIS SECOND GOAL ON HIS DEBUT V VILLA

ANTONIO'S SWIMMING CELEBRATION AGAINST THE CLARETS

47

WEST HAM UNITED
LONDON

ANTONIO BEATS TOTTENHAM'S
HUGO LLORIS TO SCORE THE OPENER
AT LONDON STADIUM

ISSA DIOP SCORES THE SECOND
AGAINST THE BLADES

LINGARD SCORES GOAL
NUMBER TWO V SPURS

Any hopes of FA Cup glory were extinguished in the fifth round as the Hammers bowed out to Manchester United after extra-time at Old Trafford.

A straightforward 3-0 home win over bottom side Sheffield United was then followed by goals from Antonio and Lingard which secured a vital victory over London rivals Tottenham Hotspur at the London Stadium. February's fixtures concluded with a narrow 2-1 defeat at league leaders Manchester City.

First-half goals from Lingard and Craig Dawson saw the Irons complete a league double over Leeds United before once again going down narrowly at Manchester United. March ended in frustrating fashion as the Hammers let a three-goal lead slip against Arsenal as two points were dropped in the pursuit of European football.

With the side firmly in the fight for a top-six finish, and with it the reward of European action for 2021/22, April proved to be something of a mixed bag for those of a claret and blue persuasion. Two thrilling 3-2 victories over Wolves (away) and Leicester City (home) were then followed by an agonising 3-2 defeat at Newcastle and a 1-0 loss at home to Chelsea.

After ending April on the back of two defeats, Moyes' men once again showed their character as they came from behind to win 2-1 at Burnley thanks to a Turf Moor brace from Antonio. Everton then avenged their 1-0 New Year's Day defeat to the Hammers with a 1-0 away triumph of their own.

A late Said Benrahma goal saw West Ham take a point from a trip to Brighton before they concluded their away fixtures with a 3-1 win at West Bromwich Albion. A successful campaign then concluded with a 3-0 final-day victory over Southampton in front of a limited crowd of 10,000 at London Stadium.

Despite all the difficulties that the pandemic provided, West Ham United rose to the challenge that the 2020/21 season presented and successfully secured a top-six Premier League finish. Not only did the team win a club record 65 points at Premier League level, but they also set new records for the number of Premier League games won in a season (19) and the number of away victories (9).

Manager Moyes and his players will now be relishing the chance to go again in 2021/22 and with their loyal supporters in attendance both home and away as the club competes in both domestic and European football.

BOWEN JUBILANT AFTER SCORING THE WINNER V LEICESTER CITY AT LONDON STADIUM

SAID BENRAHMA NETS AT BRIGHTON

49

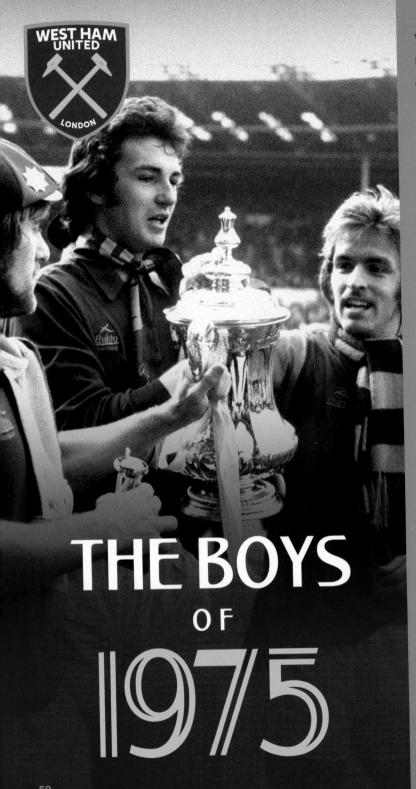

THE BOYS
OF
1975

West Ham United won their first trophy under the guidance of manager John Lyall as the club lifted the FA Cup for a second time in 1974/75.

The Hammers secured a respectable mid-table finish in the First Division, but again it was the FA Cup that really sparked the imagination of the supporters.

The Road to Wembley began with a 2-1 win away to Second Division Southampton in the third round. Just as in their cup triumph eleven years earlier, the Hammers once again faced Swindon Town - this time at the fourth round stage. After being held to a surprise 1-1 draw at the Boleyn Ground by the Third Division Robins, Lyall's men faced a tough trip to the County Ground for the replay. A hard-fought 2-1 win in Wiltshire subsequently teed-up a fifth-round London derby at home to Queens Park Rangers.

In front of a bumper Boleyn crowd of 39,193, the Hammers secured a quarter-final spot with a 2-1 win.

The quarter-final draw saw West Ham handed another London derby as they headed to Highbury to face Arsenal. In what was only his fifth appearance and second start in a West Ham shirt, following a £40,000 transfer from Rochdale, Alan Taylor swiftly won the hearts of the West Ham fans as he scored both goals in an epic 2-0 victory.

Taylor was once again the two-goal hero as the Hammers booked their place in the final. After the initial semi-final against Ipswich Town at Villa Park had ended goalless, Taylor netted twice in the Stamford Bridge replay as the Irons came from behind to seal a 2-1 win and book a Wembley date with Second Division Fulham.

After two goals in the quarter-final and a second brace in the semi-final success at Stamford Bridge, Taylor's magic touch in the cup continued as he proceeded to score twice in the final. On target after 60 and 64 minutes, his goals ensured West Ham defeated a Fulham side that included former Hammers captain Bobby Moore and former England man Alan Mullery.

It was skipper Billy Bonds who led the team up the famous Wembley steps to collect the trophy as Bonds and his teammates entered the record books as being the last all-English team to win the FA Cup.

WEST HAM
UNITED

LONDON

STAR MAN
ALAN TAYLOR

Alan Taylor will forever be remembered for his FA Cup goalscoring heroics in 1974/75. With two goals in the Wembley Final, Taylor's name is embedded in West Ham United folklore.

Proving his cup scoring exploits of 1974/75 were not a one off, Taylor continued his fine form in front of goal when he was the club's leading scorer in 1975/76. He ended the campaign with 17 goals and was on target in the memorable European Cup Winners' Cup campaign - netting goals against Ararat Erevan and Den Haag.

In total, Alan Taylor scored 36 goals for West Ham United in 124 games between December 1974 and May 1979.

ALAN TAYLOR SCORES

BILLY BONDS, BOBBY MOORE & GRAHAM PADDON

KEVIN LOCK, ALAN TAYLOR & BOBBY GOULD

51

CLASSIC
FAN'TASTIC

Five West Ham United FA Cup-winning stars are hiding in the 1975 Wembley crowd. Can you find them?

ANSWERS ON PAGE 82 53

REWIND
QUIZ OF THE YEAR

With the Covid-19 pandemic resulting in the majority of the 2020/21 football season being played behind closed, what can you recall of the Hammers' on-pitch action from the 2020/21 campaign?

01

Against which League One opponent did Sebastien Haller score a pre season hat-trick?

06

Which player netted a dramatic injury-time equaliser against Tottenham Hotspur as the Hammers came from 3-0 down to salvage a point in October 2020?

From which club did the Hammers sign Tomas Soucek in July 2020?

02

04

Which London club were West Ham paired with in the second round of the League Cup?

07

Who kept goal for the Hammers in their 5-1 League Cup third round victory over Hull City?

09

Can you name the player who scored his last goal for the club in the League Cup match away to Everton?

Who took the mantle of scoring West Ham's first Premier League goal of 2020/21?

03

05

Can you name the Crystal Palace striker who scored against the Hammers at London Stadium in December 2020, but was later sent off?

08

At which away venue did the Hammers record their first Premier League away clean sheet of the season?

10

Who were West Ham's final opponents of the 2020 calendar year?

54

11

In January 2021, which non-league club were the Hammers paired with in the third round of the FA Cup?

13

Who were the opposition when the Hammers briefly welcomed 2,000 fans back to London Stadium for a test event in December 2020?

12

How many players were ever-present in the club's 2020/21 Premier League campaign?

14

Against which Premier League club did Jesse Lingard enjoy a two-goal debut for the Hammers when on loan from Manchester United?

16

Michail Antonio and Tomas Soucek both scored ten Premier League goals for the Hammers in 2020/21, but which player hit double figures first?

15

Who scored what proved to be the Hammers' winning goal in April's 3-2 victory over Wolverhampton Wanderers at Molineux?

17

West Ham faced the same opening-day opponent in the Premier League in 2020/21 as they did in 2021/22. True or false?

19

With how many points did the Hammers end their 2020/21 Premier League campaign?

18

West Ham won a record number of Premier League away games in 20/21. How many times did they collect all three points on the road?

20

How many Premier League points did the Hammers drop against the three relegated clubs in 2020/21?

ANSWERS ON PAGE 82

A highly impressive Premier League performer for Brighton & Hove Albion in 2020/21, central defender Ben White joined Arsenal for a reported £50M fee ahead of the new 2021/22 campaign.

Last season, White's quality and consistent performances at club level saw him called into England's provisional 33-man squad for the delayed Euro2020 finals.

Then following assured displays and two clean sheets for the Three Lions in pre-tournament victories over Austria and Romania, he was included in the final 26-man squad for the finals following an injury to Liverpool's Trent Alexander-Arnold.

Having gained valuable experience with loan spells at Newport County, Peterborough United and Leeds United, White appears to have all the qualities to add a real touch of class to the Gunners' backline.

BEN WHITE
ARSENAL

PREMIER LEAGUE
KEY PLAYERS

Once again the 2021/22 Premier League campaign appears all set to be as exciting as ever with West Ham United fans relishing being back inside London Stadium and seeing their heroes take on some of the very best players in the world. Here are 19 stars the Hammers may come face-to-face with over the coming weeks and months.

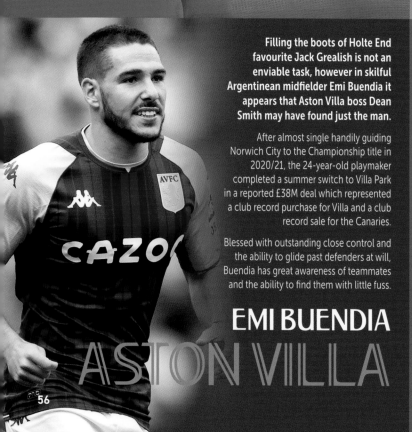

Filling the boots of Holte End favourite Jack Grealish is not an enviable task, however in skilful Argentinean midfielder Emi Buendia it appears that Aston Villa boss Dean Smith may have found just the man.

After almost single handily guiding Norwich City to the Championship title in 2020/21, the 24-year-old playmaker completed a summer switch to Villa Park in a reported £38M deal which represented a club record purchase for Villa and a club record sale for the Canaries.

Blessed with outstanding close control and the ability to glide past defenders at will, Buendia has great awareness of teammates and the ability to find them with little fuss.

EMI BUENDIA
ASTON VILLA

IVAN TONEY
BRENTFORD

A goalscoring sensation across two seasons for Peterborough United in League One, striker Ivan Toney joined Brentford in August 2021 and immediately fired the goals that won Brentford promotion to the Premier League.

Toney netted a Championship record 31 league goals last season and then added to his tally with two further strikes in the Bees' successful Play-Off campaign.

An ace penalty taker, Toney is blessed with pace, power and great off the ball movement which make him something of a defender's worst nightmare. As Brentford's go-to man for goals, a great deal will be expected of Toney if the Premier League new boys are to survive in the top flight.

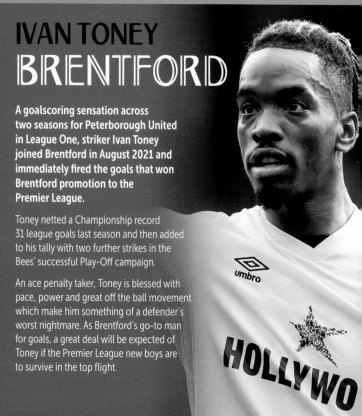

Ace marksman Chris Wood collected Burnley's Player of the Season accolade for 2020/21 after hitting double figures for the fourth consecutive season.

Signed from Leeds United in the summer of 2017, Wood has proved to be an instant success at Turf Moor and has now netted half a century of goals for the club. His goals have clearly been vital in the Clarets establishing themselves as a Premier League team.

Last season saw the Kiwi net a first Clarets' hat-trick as Burnley turned on the style to register an emphatic 4-0 victory over Wolves at Molineux in April. He will once again be the man that opposition defenders need to keep tabs on when facing Sean Dyche's side.

CHRIS WOOD
BURNLEY

Powerful Belgium international centre-forward Romelu Lukaku rejoined Chelsea in August from Inter Milan in a £97.5M transfer and marked his second Blues' debut with a goal in a London derby against Arsenal.

Now Belgium's all-time record goalscorer, Lukaku first joined Chelsea back in 2011 from Anderlecht. Following highly impressive spells at WBA, Everton and Manchester United, the threat posed by Lukaku is well known to Premier League opposition.

Lukaku's return to Stamford Bridge has seen many pundits tip Chelsea to follow up their Champions League triumph with Premier League success in 2021/22.

ROMELU LUKAKU
CHELSEA

NEAL MAUPAY
BRIGHTON & HA

A former France under-21 international, striker Neal Maupay rose to prominence with a goal-laden two-season spell at Brentford.

Brighton swooped for the Frenchman's services in August 2019 and he marked his Seagulls' debut with a goal on the opening day of the 2019/20 season as Graham Potter's side won 3-0 at Watford.

Maupay hit ten Premier League goals for Brighton in his first season at the Amex Stadium and topped the Seagulls' scoring charts again last season with eight. The 25-year-old poacher made a highly impressive start to the current 2021/22 season with a goal in each of his side's opening two Premier League fixtures as Albion defeated Burnley and Watford.

Former Chelsea defender Marc Guehi shot to prominence with a highly successful loan spell at Swansea City, which in turn led to this summer's big money move to Crystal Palace.

A member of England's U17 World Cup-winning squad, Guehi made his professional debut for Chelsea in an EFL Cup tie against Grimsby Town in 2019 and he ended the 2019/20 season with his first loan spell at Swansea.

He returned to South Wales on loan for the 2020/21 season and was ever-present as the Swans reached the Championship Play-Off final. After a series of exceptional performances for Swansea, the classy defender became Palace's third most expensive signing when he joined the Eagles in a reported £18M deal.

MARC GUEHI
CRYSTAL PALACE

Plucked from Sheffield United in 2016 for a bargain transfer fee of £1.5M, striker Dominic Calvert-Lewin was an outstanding performer for Everton last season.

The 24-year-old netted 16 Premier League goals and his impressive club form won him international recognition with England. He made his Three Lions debut in a friendly match against Wales and marked the occasion with a goal.

Part of England's Euro 2020 campaign, Dominic began the current season in fine form with goal in each of the Toffees' opening three Premier League games. After scoring four goals against the Hammers last season, David Moyes' men will be all too aware of his qualities when they face Everton in 2021/22.

DOMINIC CALVERT-LEWIN
EVERTON

KALVIN PHILLIPS
LEEDS UNITED

Kalvin Phillips followed up an outstanding 2020/21 Premier League debut season for Leeds United with a series of sensational performances for England in the Euro 2020 finals.

Very much the local hero at Elland Road, Phillips has progressed though the Leeds United Academy system and made his first-team debut back in 2015. He has now made over 200 appearances for the club and become a vital component in Marcelo Bielsa's side.

After 29 Premier League outings for the Yorkshire club, the all-action midfield dynamo then played in all seven of the Three Lions' Euro 2020 games as Gareth Southgate's side ended the tournament as runners-up.

Widely regarded as one of the very best goalkeepers in the Premier League, Kasper Schmeichel produced a heroic performance in the 2021 FA Cup final to ensure that the Foxes maintained their lead and brought the cup back to Leicester for the first time.

Following another highly impressive season at the King Power, Schmeichel was then a star performer for Denmark who reached the semi-finals of Euro 2020. The giant Dane has now amassed over 400 appearances for Leicester City since joining the club in 2011.

He has also topped the 70-appearance mark at international level, but remains someway short of his father Peter's record 129 caps for the Danes.

KASPER SCHMEICHEL
LEICESTER CITY

Portuguese international Bruno Fernandes made an instant impact at Old Trafford following his January 2020 signing from Sporting Lisbon.

The highly-skilful midfielder's arrival certainly sparked an upturn in United's fortunes and despite only being at the club for half the campaign, supporters voted him their Player of the Season for 2019/20.

He ended last season as the Red Devil's top scorer with 18 Premier League goals and began the current campaign in sensational form when he netted a hat-trick in the Red Devils' 5-1 thrashing of Leeds United at Old Trafford on the opening day.

BRUNO FERNANDES
MAN UTD

A cool and commanding presence at the heart of the Liverpool defence, Dutch international central-defender Virgil van Dijk proved to be the missing part of the jigsaw as Liverpool finally ended their long wait for the Premier League title in 2019/20.

With great pace, superb tackling skills and a wonderful ability to read the game, van Dijk is clearly a calming influence on the Reds' defensive unit.

An injury suffered in the Merseyside derby at Everton in October 2020 ruled him out for the remainder of the season and effectively ended any hopes the Reds had of retaining their title, but Liverpool fans were delighted to see their key man return when they opened the 2021/22 campaign with a 3-0 victory at newly-promoted Norwich City.

VIRGIL VAN DIJK
LIVERPOOL

All eyes will be on Manchester City's England midfielder Jack Grealish this season following his British record £100M transfer to the Etihad Stadium from Aston Villa in August 2021.

Blessed with wonderful close control and sublime dribbling skills, Grealish can glide past opponents with little fuss. He also has an exceptional eye for a pass and the ability to unlock the tightest of defences.

A lifelong Villa fan and having first joined the club as a six-year-old, it was clearly a big decision for the 26-year-old to leave Villa Park. However, he wasted little time in making an impact with City as he marked his home debut with the champions' second goal in a 5-0 rout of Norwich City.

JACK GREALISH
MAN CITY

England U21 midfielder Joe Willock joined Newcastle United at the start of the 2021/22 Premier League season after a highly-successful loan spell at St James' Park.

After progressing though the Arsenal Academy and scoring eleven goals in 78 appearances for the Gunners, Willock joined Newcastle United on loan in February 2021 for the remainder of the 2020/21 campaign. A remarkable return of eight goals from 14 Premier League appearances saw a clamour for a permanent move to the north east.

The Newcastle fans were delighted when Willock agreed a six-year deal with the Magpies Park following a reported £25M transfer.

JOE WILLOCK
NEWCASTLE UTD

A Man of the Match performance for Scotland in their Euro 2020 finals draw with England at Wembley enhanced the growing reputation of Chelsea midfielder Billy Gilmour.

The 20-year-old midfielder maestro agreed a season-long loan with Premier League new boys Norwich City in June 2021 and made his debut for the Canaries in their opening Premier League match with Liverpool.

Clearly a young player with massive potential, Gilmour already has Premier League, Champions League and international experience. The Scot's progress at Carrow Road over the 2021/22 campaign could well play a massive part in the Canaries' chances of Premier League survival.

BILLY GILMOUR
NORWICH CITY

ADAM ARMSTRONG
SOUTHAMPTON

Adam Armstrong wasted little time in introducing himself to the Saints fans as he marked his Southampton debut with a goal against Everton on the opening day of the new 2021/22 season.

An exciting summer signing from Blackburn Rovers, where he scored 28 goals at Championship level last season, 24-year-old Armstrong agreed a four-year deal at St Mary's in August 2021 as the Saints looked to replace the goal threat they lost following Danny Ings' transfer to Aston Villa.

Armstrong has Premier League experience having begun his career at Newcastle United. A reliable finisher in one-on-one situations, Armstrong also has the ability to cut in from wide areas and create goals of his own.

South Korean international Son Heung-min joined Tottenham Hotspur back in 2015 from Bayer Leverkusen and has established himself as one of the Premier League most feared strikers.

An extremely popular character with supporters and teammates alike, Son's goalscoring partnership with England captain Harry Kane helped Spurs reach the Champions League final in 2019.

The 2021/22 campaign will be the 29-year-olds seventh season in the Premier League. He has already netted over a century of goals for Spurs and his first strike of the season secured a memorable 1-0 opening-day victory at home to champions Manchester City.

SON HEUNG-MIN
SPURS

Closing in on 300 appearances for Wolverhampton Wanderers, defender Conor Coady has enjoyed phenomenal success at Molineux following his 2014 move from Huddersfield Town.

With the ability to operate as one of a pair of central defenders or as one of a three, Coady has been the model of consistency for Wolves and was ever-present throughout the club's first two season back in the Premier League in 2018/19 and 2019/20.

Captain of the Molineux side, Coady's club form has been rewarded with five full England caps and the 28-year-old was a member of England's successful Euro 2020 squad.

CONOR COADY
WOLVES

Flying wide-man Ismaila Sarr played a vital part in Watford's instant return to the Premier League in 2020/21 and could well be the Hornets' one to watch in 2021/22.

The Senegal international scored 13 goals as the Hornets secured the runners-up spot in the Championship and on top of his goals, he also registered five assists for teammates. He was also the Championship's most fouled player as opposition defenders continually failed to get to grips with his threat.

Fittingly, Sarr was on target as Watford began life back in the Premier League with a thrilling 3-2 opening-day victory over Aston Villa at Vicarage Road.

ISMAILA SARR
WATFORD

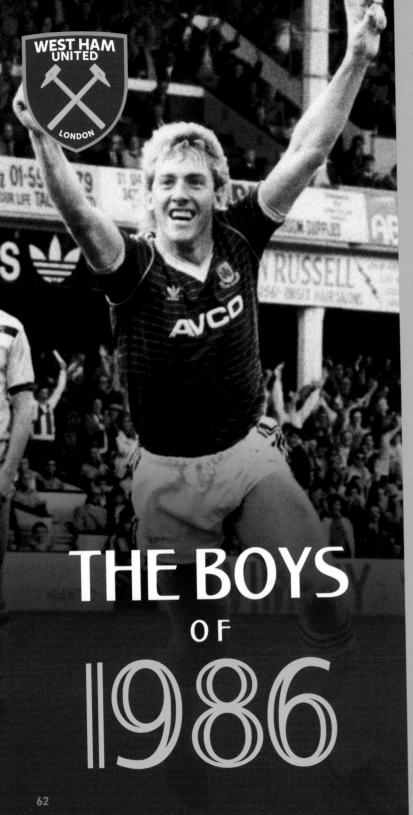

THE BOYS
OF
1986

After a somewhat underwhelming 16th-place end to their 1984/85 First Division campaign, few at the Boleyn Ground anticipated what was in store for West Ham United in 1985/86.

For a club whose proud history is peppered with exciting cup runs, the Hammers' 1985/86 season was all about their league campaign.

Manager John Lyall introduced two summer signings to his opening-day line-up away to Birmingham City with former Oldham Athletic midfielder Mark Ward and St Mirren striker Frank McAvennie both handed debuts at St Andrew's. A 1-0 defeat was far from an ideal start to the season, but once back on home soil things swiftly began to take shape.

McAvennie, who had played in midfield on his debut, was paired with home-grown hero Tony Cottee in attack and a formidable strike partnership was born. McAvennie marked his home debut with a brace in a 3-1 victory over Queens Park Rangers. In tandem with Cottee, the pair would go on to net an incredible 46 league goals between them as the Hammers engaged in a three-way battle for the First Division title with Merseyside rivals Liverpool and Everton.

A brace each from McAvennie and Cottee inspired a 4-1 home win over Aston Villa on 19 October 1985 and that triggered a run of nine straight top-flight victories which propelled the Hammers into the title race. At the end of November, West Ham were third in the table, five points behind leaders Manchester United and McAvennie was the Football League's leading marksman with 17 goals.

In February, West Ham defeated Manchester United 2-1 at the Boleyn Ground, a result that saw United replaced at the summit by reigning champions Everton.

As the season progressed, a potential league and cup double looked possible, particularly after the Hammers won an FA Cup fifth-round replay at Old Trafford. Sadly, the cup dream ended at the quarter-final stage with a 2-1 defeat at Sheffield Wednesday. Despite a frustrating narrow 2-1 reverse at Nottingham Forest in early April, the Hammers recovered to win eight of their next nine league games including an 8-1 demolition of Newcastle United.

The Irons' penultimate game of the season was won 3-2 at WBA, but while the Hammers were winning at the Hawthorns, Liverpool triumphed 1-0 at Chelsea to secure the title. A final-day 3-1 defeat at Everton saw West Ham end the season in third place - the highest ever finish in the club's history.

STAR MAN
FRANK McAVENNIE

Frank McAvennie enjoyed a dream start to life at the Boleyn Ground following his £340,000 transfer from St Mirren in the summer of 1985.

The striker made an instant impression on the home faithful as he scored twice on his home debut in a 3-1 win over Queens Park Rangers as the Hammers secured their first three points of the 1985/86 campaign.

From that moment on, both McAvennie and West Ham United never looked back as John Lyall's men delivered a memorable 1985/86 campaign which saw the Scot end the season as the club's leading scorer with 26 First Division goals.

FRANK McAVENNIE WITH MANCHESTER UNITED DEFENDER KEVIN MORAN DURING THE 2-1 FIRST DIVISION VICTORY AT UPTON PARK

FRANK McAVENNIE

FRANK McAVENNIE

JOHN LYALL

TONY COTTEE

WEST HAM UNITED
LONDON

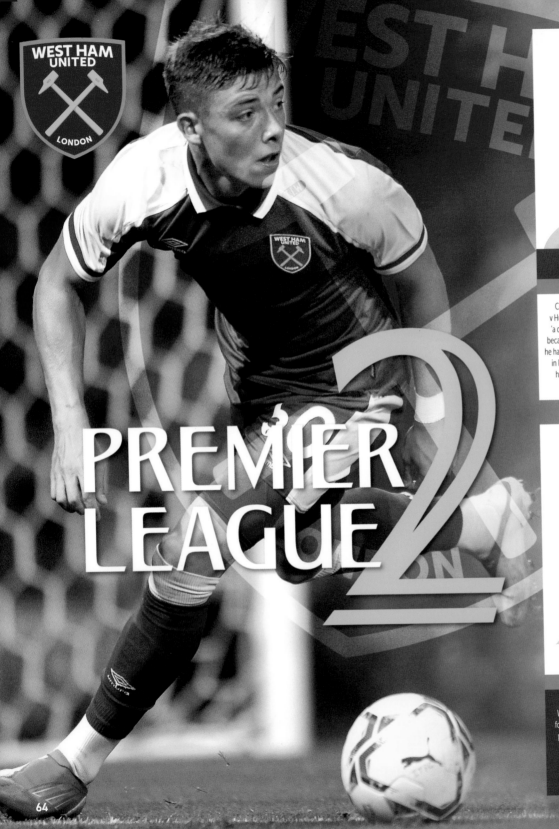

PREMIER LEAGUE 2

AJIBOLA ALESE

POSITION: Defender   **DOB:** 17/01/2001

Centre-back Ajibola Alese made his first-team debut for West Ham United v Hull City in the Carabao Cup in September 2020, describing the occasion as 'a dream come true'. Having been with the Club since the age of seven, Alese became a full-time Academy of Football scholar in summer 2017, by which time he had already made his U18 Premier League debut. He made his first appearance in Premier League 2 against Everton in August 2017 and put pen-to-paper on his first professional contract with the Irons eleven months later. Alese has been capped by England at all levels between U16 and U20.

HARRISON ASHBY

POSITION: Defender   **DOB:** 14/11/2001

Attack-minded right-back Harrison Ashby has been a regular fixture in West Ham United's development squads since the 2017/18 season. Son of the former Watford, Brentford and Gillingham defender Barry, Ashby signed his first professional contract with the Hammers in the summer of 2020. He made his senior debut for the club against Charlton Athletic in the Carabao Cup soon after and started against Hull City in the next round of the competition. A memorable 2020/21 season continued as he was called up by Scotland Under-21s for the first time.

OSSAMA ASHLEY

POSITION: Midfielder   **DOB:** 23/02/2000

By modern standards, Ossama Ashley's route into professional football happened relatively late on, as he joined Fulham's youth set-up at the age of 16. The box-to-box midfielder signed for AFC Wimbledon a year later, making his senior debut in an EFL Trophy tie against Yeovil Town in December 2017. He signed a professional contract with the Dons in March 2019, but departed just over a year later. Ashley joined West Ham United on a trial basis in August 2020 and impressed in a series of pre-season friendlies. The Hammers subsequently offered him a one-year contract that has since been extended.

AMANDOU DIALLO

POSITION: Forward   **DOB:** 15/02/2003

Amandou Diallo missed a significant period of the 2020/21 season due to an injury and made just nine appearances across the U18s and U23s. A major highlight came at the end of the campaign though, as the skilful forward received his first call-up to the England Under-19 squad. Diallo originally joined West Ham United at the age of 10, having impressed at Sunday league level. Such was his impact within the Academy of Football that he was just 14 years and six months old when he debuted in the U18 Premier League at Arsenal in August 2017.

DANIEL CHESTERS

POSITION: Midfielder   **DOB:** 04/04/2002

Attacking midfielder Daniel Chesters signed a professional contract with West Ham United in the summer of 2020, having completed a two-year scholarship with the Club. Chesters had impressed sufficiently to make his debut for the Irons U23 side in a Premier League 2 fixture against Liverpool in February 2018 prior to him starting his scholarship. His first season as a full-time U23 player saw Chesters pick up a goal and an assist in 18 appearances in Premier League 2 Division 1 and the Papa John's Trophy whilst playing in a variety of roles in midfield, and occasionally, as a full-back.

MESAQUE DJU

POSITION: Defender   **DOB:** 18/03/1999

Mesaque Dju joined West Ham United in January 2019 from Portuguese side Benfica. Born in Guinea-Bissau, Dju moved to Portugal as a boy, joining Benfica at the age of eleven. There, he was part of the squad which reached the 2017 UEFA Youth League final and were crowned Portuguese national U19 league champions for 2017/18. After injury troubles in his first two seasons with the Hammers, he featured regularly for the U23s in 2020/21, netting twice in 14 appearances.

PIERRE EKWAH

POSITION: Midfielder   **DOB: 15/01/2002**

Pierre Ekwah joined West Ham United from Chelsea in June 2021 having previously spent two weeks on trial with the Hammers. During that time, he featured in the U23s' last two Premier League 2 Division 1 matches of the 2020/21 season - both against Arsenal - which saw him score in the latter fixture. A powerful defensive midfielder also capable of dropping into the back line, Ekwah spent three years at the renowned INF Clairefontaine academy in France as a teenager. He subsequently spent a year with Ligue 1 side FC Nantes, before joining Chelsea's Academy in the summer of 2018.

KEENAN FORSON

POSITION: Midfielder   **DOB: 16/10/2001**

Energetic midfielder Keenan Forson, full name Keenan Appiah-Forson, joined West Ham United at the age of 14 on the back of a trial with the club. Forson played a key role in the Hammers' successful fight against relegation in Premier League 2 Division 1 in 2020/21, scoring three times in 17 starts for the U23s in all competitions. Usually selected in central-midfield, Forson impressed coming on as a substitute for the Hammers' U21s when asked to play at right-back against Newport County in the Football League Trophy. The Hammers won 5-4 that night having trailed 4-1 prior to Forson's introduction.

JAYDEN FEVRIER

POSITION: Defender   **DOB: 14/04/2003**

At the end of the 2020/21 season, Jayden Fevrier was presented with the Dylan Tombides Award for Best Scholar as well as the equivalent Premier League award. This came on the back a campaign in which he played a pivotal role in the U23s' successful battle against relegation in Premier League 2 Division 1. Fevrier has been with the club since the age of six, making his debut in the U18 Premier League at the age of 15 years and seven months in November 2017, while he made his first U23s appearance less than a year later.

WILL GREENIDGE

POSITION: Defender   **DOB: 15/05/2002**

Will Greenidge was a model of consistency for West Ham United's U18s during the 2019/20, as he made 20 appearances and scooped the Dylan Tombides Award. Having missed just one match for the U18s all the season, the defender signed his first professional contract in the summer of 2020. The 2020/21 campaign was far more disappointing as injury restricted him to just seven appearances across Premier League 2 and the Papa John's Trophy in his inaugural season as a full-time U23 player.

KRISZTIAN HEGYI

POSITION: Goalkeeper   **DOB: 24/09/2002**

Hungarian goalkeeper Krisztian Hegyi joined the Academy of Football in May 2019 after the Hammers beat off competition from a number of high-profile clubs for his signature. His West Ham United U18 debut came against Brighton & Hove Albion in April 2019 while he made his bow for the U23s during the 2019/20 season. Hegyi recorded 19 appearances in total across U18 Premier League South and the FA Youth Cup during the 2020/21 campaign and was nominated for the Under-18 Save of the Season at the Premier League's Academy Awards for an outstanding stop in a match against Crystal Palace in April 2021.

BRIAN KINNEAR

POSITION: Goalkeeper   **DOB: 16/01/2001**

Scotland U21 international goalkeeper Brian Kinnear joined West Ham United in the summer of 2021 after completing a successful trial with the Academy of Football. After coming through the ranks at Rangers, Kinnear was named as a member of Steven Gerrard's UEFA Europa League squad during the 2020/21 campaign. The keeper played for Rangers' youth and B sides and also enjoyed senior experience during loan spells with East of Scotland Premier Division club Camelon Juniors and Scottish League Two side Annan Athletic during his time at Ibrox.

PREMIER LEAGUE 2

WEST HAM UNITED
LONDON

PREMIER LEAGUE 2

EMMANUEL LONGELO

POSITION: Forward   **DOB:** 27/12/2000

Emmanuel Longelo came off the bench to make his senior West Ham United debut in the 5-1 win over Hull City in the Carabao Cup in September 2020. The attack-minded full-back, who originally joined the Academy of Football at the age of nine, played the most minutes of any member of the Hammers' U23s squad in 2020/21. He featured in 25 matches across the Premier League 2 and the Papa John's Trophy, recording five assists in the process. He was awarded a new long-term contract in May 2021.

THIERRY NEVERS

POSITION: Forward   **DOB:** 26/03/2002

Promising young forward Thierry Nevers joined West Ham United from Reading on a three-year contract in June 2021. Typically operating as a left-winger, Nevers is also comfortable playing through the middle. Nevers enjoyed a fruitful career at Reading, regularly featuring for the Royals at U18 and U23 level. He netted nine times in 25 appearances in Premier League 2, which included a strike against the Hammers in a 3-3 draw in January 2020.

LEVI LAING

POSITION: Defender   **DOB:** 12/04/2003

Levi Laing joined West Ham United in January 2021 and made an instant impact at the Academy of Football with 13 appearances for the youth team and two for the U23s in his maiden half-season. Around six months later, he signed his first professional contract with the club. Raised in Kingston, south west London, Laing played football for local team Hampton & Richmond Borough FC as a youngster. He started training with Brentford from the age of 12 before joining Arsenal's academy two years later, where he stayed for some five seasons.

ARMSTRONG OKOFLEX

POSITION: Forward   **DOB:** 02/03/2002

Irish winger Armstrong Okoflex signed a two-year contract with West Ham United in the summer of 2021 upon the expiration of his deal at Scottish giants, Celtic. The Republic of Ireland U19 international enjoyed a successful trial at the Academy of Football at the end of the 2020/21 season, making a positive impression on his now-teammates and coaches. The Dubliner was named in his first senior Celtic matchday squad as a 16-year-old before making his first-team debut in January 2021 with a 30-minute appearance against Hibernian.

BERNARDO ROSA

POSITION: Midfielder   **DOB:** 20/09/2000

Joining the Academy of Football in his early teenage years, Brazilian Bernardo Rosa had previously trained with Vasco da Gama and CR Flamengo in his homeland before his move to London. Having progressed through the academy ranks, Rosa wowed during the 2019/20 season, playing more minutes than any other young Hammer in the club's Premier League 2 Division 2 title-winning campaign. During the season, he was named among David Moyes' substitutes for the Premier League trip to Sheffield United in January 2020. He made 19 appearances for the U23 in 2020/21.

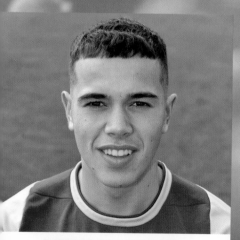

LENNON PEAKE

POSITION: Midfielder   **DOB:** 22/07/2002

A long-term injury meant Lennon Peake was unable to make any appearances during the 2020/21 season, but everyone at the Academy of Football is already well aware of his ability. The winger made the step up to youth-team level when he signed a two-year scholarship in the summer of 2018. He made his U18 Premier League debut as a substitute in the 4-1 win away to Fulham in September 2018 and featured against Tottenham Hotspur three weeks later before injury ruled him out for the rest of the campaign. He made eleven U18 Premier League South appearances in 2019/20.

KAMARAI SWYER

POSITION: Midfielder   **DOB:** 04/12/2002

A member of the Academy of Football since the age of eight, Kamarai Swyer put pen-to-paper on his first professional contract on his 18th birthday in December 2020. Swyer enjoyed an excellent first year as an U18s scholar, netting five times in just eleven appearances in the league during 2019/20. He started the following season as a regular in Kevin Keen's U18s team while he made his U23s and Premier League 2 debut as a substitute against Blackburn Rovers in October 2020. He finished the season having made 10 Premier League 2 appearances and 17 for the U18s while he also featured in the EFL Trophy.

PREMIIER
LEAGUE QUIZ
20 TEASERS
TO TACKLE ON THE 2021/22 PREMIER LEAGUE CLUBS

06

Romelu Lukaku joined Chelsea for a second time in August 2021 when he signed from Inter Milan, but which club did he leave to first join the Blues in 2011?

01

Ahead of which Premier League season did Arsenal move to the Emirates Stadium?

02

Prior to this summer's record signing of Emi Buendia from Norwich City, who was Aston Villa's previous record signing?

04

At which venue will Brighton & Hove Albion play a competitive league fixture for the first time in 2021/22?

07

Crystal Palace manager Patrick Vieira is famed for his playing career with Arsenal, but which other Premier side has Vieira played for?

Who was the last man to manage Leeds United in the Premier League before Marcelo Bielsa?

09

03

Brentford are competing in the Premier League for the first time in 2021/22, but when were the Bees last in the top-flight?

05

With which country has Burnley striker Chris Wood won over fifty international caps?

08

Prior to Dominic Calvert-Lewin, who was the last Everton player to score for England?

10

How many other current Premier League clubs has Leicester City boss Brendan Rodgers managed?

11

From which club did Liverpool sign the Premier League goalscoring sensation Mohamed Salah?

13

Can you name the Manchester United and England under-21 international full-back who has been loaned to a Premier League club for 2021/22?

16

Southampton signed striker Adam Armstrong from Blackburn Rovers ahead of the 2021/22 season, but at which Premier League club did he begin his career?

12

Who scored the dramatic late final-day goal that won Manchester City their first Premier League title in 2011/12?

14

Newcastle's summer signing Joe Willock enjoyed a successful loan spell at St James' Park before joining the Magpies permanently.

How many Premier League goals did Willock score while on loan last season - 8, 9 or 10?

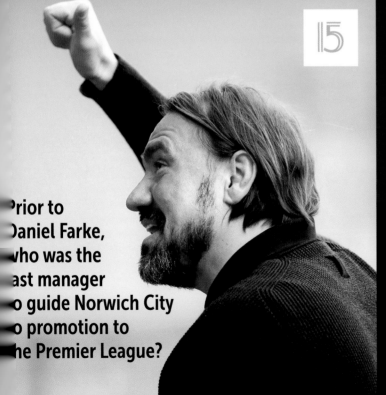

15

Prior to Daniel Farke, who was the last manager to guide Norwich City to promotion to the Premier League?

17

Other than Spurs, which other club has Harry Kane played Premier League football for?

18

During Watford's last Premier League campaign in 2019/20, how many different managers did the Hornets have?

19

Can you name the current Match of the Day pundit who scored his last Premier League goal for West Ham United?

20

Prior to Conor Coady who was Wolves' last Premier League player to play for England?

ANSWERS ON PAGE 82

THE HAMMERS ACADEMY

JAMAL BAPTISTE

POSITION: Defender   **DOB:** 11/11/2003

2020/21 saw Jamal Baptiste gain first-team involvement, as he featured in the 5-1 pre-season win over Wycombe Wanderers. He was a regular for the U23s with 23 appearances in all competitions while he made his competitive senior debut in the 4-0 FA Cup victory at Doncaster Rovers. He trained with the first-team in the summer of 2021, scoring in pre-season at Dundee. The defender has been capped at U17 and U18 level by England.

BILLY BATES

POSITION: Defender   **DOB:** 25/09/2004

Hertfordshire-born centre-back Billy Bates showed great determination and discipline to recover from a long-term knee injury prior to signing for West Ham United from Norwich City in September 2020. Bates, who also previously plied his trade for Leyton Orient, is a ball-playing defender who reads the game well. He featured in three U18 Premier League matches for the Hammers in 2020/21.

KAELAN CASEY

POSITION: Defender   **DOB:** 28/10/2004

The 2020/21 season saw Kaelan Casey make four appearances for West Ham United's U18s whilst still a schoolboy. The centre-back, who has been a member of the Academy of Football since the age of five, cites Declan Rice as his footballing inspiration. Casey made his non-competitive U23s debut in pre-season in the 4-1 win against Loughborough University in July 2021.

REGAN CLAYTON

POSITION: Defender   **DOB:** 11/11/2004

Regan Clayton was a regular for West Ham United's U18s during the 2020/21 season, making 17 appearances in the U18 Premier League in which he made two assists. He also featured in two A Youth Cup matches, including the 5-0 victory over Norwich City at Carrow Road. A flying left-back, who loves nothing more than joining in with attacking moves, Clayton's game is inspired by Bayern Munich full-back Alphonso Davies.

GEORGE EARTHY

POSITION: Midfielder   **DOB:** 05/09/2004

Despite being an U16s player, George Earthy was an U18s regular for West Ham United in 2020/21, making 16 appearances in all competitions. Capable of playing anywhere across the midfield, including deep-lying positions, out wide or as an advanced playmaker, Earthy scored four times in the final five games of the U18 Premier League South campaign. The player has previously been capped by England at U16 level.

ASHER FALASE

POSITION: Defender   **DOB:** 13/10/2004

Raised in Harlow, Essex, Asher Falase joined West Ham United as a nine-year-old and signed scholarship forms with the club ahead of the start of the 2021/22 season. An attack-minded full-back, who is also known for his tough tackling, Asher made three appearances for the U18s in 2020/21 as his development in the Claret and Blue continued.

REMY CODDINGTON

POSITION: Midfielder   **DOB:** 03/06/2004

Remy Coddington signed a full-time scholarship at the Academy of Football in July 2020, having joined the club from AFC Bournemouth. The midfielder, who started his career with North Village Rams in his native Bermuda made his senior international debut for the islands nation in March 2021, scoring in a 3-0 win over the Bahamas. Coddington made his first appearances for the Hammers U18s against Tottenham Hotspur in September 2020.

ISAAC EVANS

POSITION: Defender   **DOB:** 09/09/2003

Formerly on the books at Watford, Isaac Evans joined the Academy of Football in July 2020. The left-back made his U18 Premier League South debut against Tottenham Hotspur in September 2020 during an injury-plagued campaign that saw him play ten matches in the division overall. Renowned for his quality in wide areas, Evans has set himself a target of adding goals to his game in the youth team going forward.

MICHAEL FORBES

POSITION: Defender   **DOB:** 29/04/2004

Michael Forbes honed his skills as a footballer with the likes of Cookstown Youth and Dungannon Swifts in his native Northern Ireland prior to signing a two-year scholarship deal the Hammers in the summer of 2020. An impressive first season in 2020/21 saw the left-footed centre-back make 19 appearances for the Hammers' youth team. He also made his development squad debut in the 1-0 win over Portsmouth's first-team in the Papa John's Trophy in November 2020.

THE HAMMERS ACADEMY

GIDEON KODUA

POSITION: Forward　　**DOB: 02/10/2004**

Gideon Kadua joined the Academy of Football in 2017 having been spotted playing for Newham District. The skilful right-winger completed a successful six-week trial at the club, which included a goalscoring appearance against Luton Town. The scholar made his U18s debut in the 4-1 win over Reading in April 2021, while he made substitute appearances against Reading and Crystal Palace early on in the 2021/22 U18 Premier League South season.

DIVIN MUBAMA

POSITION: Striker　　**DOB: 25/10/2004**

Divin Mubama was the Hammers U18's top scorer in 2020/21, netting 11 times in 25 appearances, including a hat-trick against Reading in a 4-1 win in April 2021 just days after he was called up for England U17s. Raised in Canning Town, Mubama joined the Academy of Football as an eight-year-old left-back, eventually becoming a striker. Prior to the suspension of Academy football in 2019/20, he had 45 goals for the season to his name for that campaign.

JACOB KNIGHTBRIDGE

POSITION: Goalkeeper　　**DOB: 25/01/2004**

Brentwood born and raised, Jacob Knightbridge originally joined West Ham United at the age of seven. The goalkeeper, who has represented England at U17 level, became a scholar with the club during the summer of 2020. He made four appearances for Kevin Keen's U18s in 2020/21 and also took his place amongst the substitutes for the U23s' trips to Tottenham Hotspur and Arsenal in Premier League 2.

SONNY PERKINS

POSITION: Midfielder　　**DOB: 10/02/2004**

Sonny Perkins joined the Irons at the end of the U14s phase from Leyton Orient. Hackney born and raised, Perkins was part of the Orient set-up from the age of eight. He signed a scholarship deal with the Hammers in the summer of 2020, ahead of a phenomenal season for the young playmaker who netted five times in 28 appearances for the U18s in 2020/21. Perkins scored a hat-trick for England U16s in a 4-1 win over the United States in February 2020.

FREDDIE POTTS

POSITION: Midfielder **DOB: 12/09/2003**

Son of West Ham legend Steve and brother of ex-Hammer and current Luton Town left-back Dan, Freddie Potts joined the Academy of Football at the age of six. He signed his first professional contract with the club in June 2021, having put pen-to-paper on a scholarship deal only a year earlier. Potts scored once in 21 U18 Premier League appearances in 2020/21 while he also netted once in 8 Premier League 2 matches during the campaign.

LAURENCE SHALA

POSITION: Goalkeeper **DOB: 11/09/2004**

London born and raised, Laurence Shala joined West Ham United's pre-Academy as a five-year-old and signed for the Club four years later. He made his debut for Kosovo at U19s in June 2021, having previously represented them at U15 and U17 level. His Hammers youth team debut arrived three months earlier, as he started in the 2-1 U18 Premier League victory over Leicester City at Rush Green.

MASON TERRY

POSITION: Goalkeeper **DOB: 20/09/2004**

Mason Terry joined West Ham as a nine-year-old, having been spotted playing for Sunday League side Essex Allstars. The goalkeeper, who is from Canvey Island, ran 70km around his local area in seven days back in May 2020, to raise funds for the Mid & South Essex Hospitals Charity during the initial coronavirus nationwide lockdown. An U15 player at the time, Terry kept himself fit during lockdown by following the U18s' training programme.

JUNIOR ROBINSON

POSITION: Defender **DOB: 06/04/2004**

A right-sided defender who occasionally plays in midfield, Junior Robinson joined the Academy of Football as a six-year-old having been spotted playing for the renowned Sunday League team Senrab FC in Forest Gate. Robinson signed a two-year scholarship with West Ham United in the summer of 2020. He made his England U17 debut against Belgium towards the end of the year, having previously represented the Young Lions at U15 level.

SEAN TARIMA

POSITION: Defender **DOB: 12/09/2004**

Centre-back Sean Tarima, who is also comfortable playing in midfield, made his debut for West Ham United's U18s in the 1-1 draw at Leicester City in the U18 Premier League in May 2021. Born in Newham and raised in Romford, Tarima originally joined the Hammers as a nine-year-old. His accomplishments to date include representing England U16s in the UEFA U17 development tournament at St George's Park in October 2019.

ARCHIE WOODS

POSITION: Midfielder **DOB: 17/09/2003**

Archie Woods is a lifelong West Ham United supporter, who has had the honour of captaining the club at U15 and U16 level. The defensive midfielder was a regular for the Hammers U18 team during the 2020/21 season, making 23 appearances in all competitions, including three starts in the Academy's 2020/21 FA Youth Cup run. His first goal at U18 level came in 3-2 victory over Arsenal in the U18 Premier League in October 2020.

FAST FORWARD

ONE THING'S FOR CERTAIN, 2021/22 IS GOING TO BE A GREAT SEASON, BUT WHERE ARE THE TROPHIES HEADING?

SEE IF YOU AGREE WITH OUR PREDICTIONS...

PREMIER LEAGUE WINNERS

LIVERPOOL

PREMIER LEAGUE TOP SCORER

MO SALAH

PREMIER LEAGUE RUNNERS-UP

MAN CITY

RELEGATED TO THE CHAMPIONSHIP: 18TH

WOLVES

RELEGATED TO THE CHAMPIONSHIP: 19TH

ASTON VILLA

BOTTOM OF THE PREMIER LEAGUE

NEWCAST UNITED

FA CUP WINNERS

WEST HAM UNITED

FA CUP RUNNERS-UP

EVERTON

LEAGUE CUP WINNERS

LEICESTER CITY

LEAGUE CUP RUNNER

LIVERPOOL

CHAMPIONSHIP WINNERS

FULHAM

CHAMPIONSHIP RUNNERS-UP

BORO

CHAMPIONSHIP PLAY-OFF WINNERS

DERBY COUNTY

CHAMPIONSHIP TOP SCORER

ALEKSANDAR MITROVIC

FULHAM

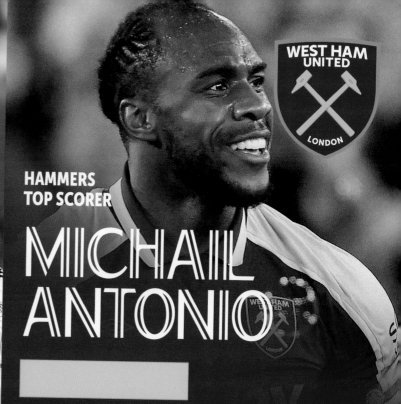

HAMMERS TOP SCORER

MICHAIL ANTONIO

HAMMER OF THE YEAR

DECLAN RICE

CHAMPIONS LEAGUE WINNERS

MAN CITY

CHAMPIONS LEAGUE RUNNERS-UP

BARCELONA

EUROPA LEAGUE WINNERS

WEST HAM UNITED

EUROPA LEAGUE RUNNERS-UP

NAPOLI

WEST HAM UNITED WOMEN

Club skipper Gilly Flaherty joined West Ham United in 2018 on the back of four years with Chelsea women and a successful spell at Arsenal. She won no fewer than 22 pieces of silverware with the Gunners and the Blues.

The centre-back was handed the Hammers' captain's armband in her first season with the club, when she played in all but one of the side's matches. She signed a new two-year deal with West Ham in 2020.

5. Gilly FLAHERTY

Capable of playing a host of different positions, including full-back, wing-back, winger and centre-forward, Perth-born Lisa Evans joined West Ham United on a season-long loan from Arsenal in August 2021.

The Scottish international has won a host of honours at club level, including four Scottish Women's Premier League titles with Glasgow City, the Bundesliga with Bayern Munich and both the FA Women's Super League and FA Women's League Cup with the Gunners.

7. Lisa EVANS

POSITION: Forward
DoB: 21/05/1992

Claudia Walker rose through the youth ranks at Stoke City prior to signing for Liverpool in 2014 - the same year as the Reds won the FA Women's Super League title.

She joined Merseyside rivals Everton in February 2015, where she won promotion to the top flight in 2017. A productive spell at Birmingham City between 2019 and 2021 preceded her arrival at West Ham United in July 2021.

9. Claudia WALKER

Having signed for West Ham United ahead of the of the 2020/21 season, Mackenzie Arnold made a total of 21 appearances for the Hammers in her debut campaign with the Club.

The Australian previously represented the likes of Perth Glory, Canberra United, Western Sydney Wanderers and Chicago Red Stars before her move to London. She was included in Australia's squad for the delayed 2020 Olympics Games, a tournament in which the Matildas finished fourth.

1. Mackenzie ARNOLD

POSITION: Goalkeeper
DoB: 25/02/1994

Four-time Czech Footballer of the Year Katerina Svitkova joined West Ham United from Slavia Prague in July 2020.

Born in Plzen, Svitkova spent her formative years as a footballer with local side Viktoria Plzen, before making the switch to Slavia Prague in 2013 as a 17-year-old, where she developed into one of Europe's finest talents. She has won over 30 caps for the Czech Republic to date and netted three times in 15 Barclays FA Women's Super League appearances for the Hammers in 2020/21.

10. Katerina SVITKOVA

POSITION: Midfielder
DoB: 20/03/1996

California-born Zaneta Wyne had prior experience of the Barclays FA Women's Super League before signing for West Ham United in June 2021, having turned out for Sunderland between 2017 and 2018.

The midfielder, who also counts San Diego WFC SeaLions, Vikingur Olafsvik, Atlanta Silverbacks and Glasgow City amongst her list of former clubs she has represented, played for current Hammers boss Olli Harder at Klepp IL between 2018 and 2019.

2. Zaneta WYNE

Lifelong Hammers fan Kate Longhurst moved to West Ham in 2018 after a five-year stint with Liverpool.

Longhurst missed just one game in her debut season with West Ham United, scoring three goals in all competitions and playing in the Women's FA Cup Final at Wembley Stadium. She continues to be a vital cog in the Hammers' midfield, featuring in 18 Barclays FA Women's Super League matches for the club during the 2020/21 campaign.

12. Kate LONGHURST

Capped by England between Under-17 and Under-23 level, Abbey-Leigh Stringer was part of the Young Lions squad that finished as runners-up at the 2013 UEFA Women's Under-19 Championships.

At club level, the midfielder has represented rivals Birmingham City and Aston Villa, while she signed for West Ham United in July 2021 from fellow Barclays FA Women's Super League side Everton.

4. Abbey-Leigh STRINGER

POSITION: Midfielder
DoB: 17/05/1995

Tameka Yallop was just nine caps short of a century of appearances for Australia at the time of writing, having been a regular in the Matildas squad since her international debut in 2007.

The midfielder has travelled to three FIFA Women's World Cups to date and was also part of Australia's squad for the 2016 and 2020 Olympic Games. She signed for West Ham United in May 2021 after spells with the likes of Brisbane Roar, Boston Breakers, FFC Frankfurt, Klepp IL and Melbourne City.

13. Tameka YALLOP

POSITION: Midfielder
DoB: 16/06/1991

Shortly after representing Japan at the delayed 2020 Olympic Games, Yui Hasegawa signed for West Ham United from Serie A side AC Milan in August 2021.

The creative midfielder put pen-to-paper on a two-year contract with the Hammers, having previously spent over a decade with Nippon TV Tokyo Verdy Beleza in her native Japan, where she rose through the youth ranks and played over 100 first-team matches.

POSITION: Midfielder
DoB: 29/01/1997
14. Yui HASEGAWA

Grace Fisk was a key member of the West Ham United squad during the 2020/21 season, playing every minute of the Barclays FA Women's Super League campaign as the Hammers avoided relegation.

Born in Bromley, Fisk moved to the United States in 2016 to study at Penn State University and, subsequently, the University of South Carolina. She played for South Carolina Gamecock prior to signing for West Ham in December 2019.

POSITION: Defender
DoB: 05/01/1998
22. Grace FISK

Born in Cambridge, Lucy Parker was a member of Arsenal's youth academy for some ten years prior to moving to the United States and the University of California at the age of 17.

Capped by England at various levels between Under-15 and Under-21, the defender signed for West Ham United in August 2021 after spells with college sides LSU Tigers and UCLA Bruins.

15. Lucy PARKER
POSITION: Defender
DoB: 18/11/1998

France international defender Hawa Cissoko joined West Ham United from ASJ Soyaux in July 2020 and made 12 appearances for the Hammers in the Barclays FA Women's Super League in her debut season in England.

Cissoko played for Paris Saint-Germain, Olympique de Marseille and Soyaux prior to her move to London. She made her senior international debut for France against Spain in September 2017.

23. Hawa CISSOKO
POSITION: Defender
DoB: 10/04/1997

Melisa Filis rose through the academy ranks at Arsenal to make her senior debut for the Gunners against Charlton Athletic during the 2018/19 season.

The midfielder departed for London Bees in September 2020, for whom she netted twice in 20 FA Women's Championship appearances. She joined West Ham United in July 2021 and was handed the number 17 shirt.

POSITION: Midfielder
DoB: 30/07/2002
17. Melisa FILIS

Previously on the books at Barclays FA Women's Super League sides Everton and Liverpool, Brooke Cairns signed for West Ham United in August 2021 at the age of 18.

Capped by England at Under-16, Under-17 and Under-18 level, Cairns was an unused substitute in the Hammers' opening match of the 2021/22 Barclays FA Women's Super League season away to Brighton & Hove Albion which left her waiting to make her senior club debut.

POSITION: Midfielder
DoB: 11/06/2003
24. Brooke CAIRNS

West Ham United bolstered their goalkeeping options in August 2021 with the signing of New Zealand international Anna Leat.

The 5' 8" stopper started her career with Auckland-based East Coast Bays before she moved to the United States to study at Georgetown University and represent college soccer side Georgetown Hoyas. She made her senior international debut in 2017 and was part of New Zealand's squad at the delayed 2020 Olympic Games.

18. Anna LEAT
POSITION: Goalkeeper
DoB: 26/06/2001

Grace Garrad joined West Ham United in August 2021 having previously been on the books at Arsenal.

The talented defender, who has represented England at Under-18 and Under-19 level, had a loan spell with FA Women's Championship side Crystal Palace during the 2020/21 season. She signed for the Hammers on the same day as former Everton and Liverpool player Brooke Cairns.

25. Grace GARRAD
POSITION: Defender
DoB: 19/06/2003

Having joined West Ham United in January 2019, Adriana Leon made ten appearances in her debut campaign for the Hammers, which included a place in the starting line-up for the 2019 FA Women's FA Cup Final.

The Canadian international followed up her three strikes in 2018/19 by netting six times in 16 matches in all competitions in 2019/20 campaign, while she made 13 appearances during an injury plagued 2020/21 season. She was part of the Canada squad that won gold at the delayed 2020 Olympic Games.

POSITION: Forward
DoB: 02/10/1992
19. Adriana LEON

Having joined West Ham United from Chelsea, Maisy Barker made her Hammers debut away to Manchester City in February 2021.

The former England Under-17 defender made a total of three Barclays FA Women's Super League appearances for the club during the 2020/21 season, featuring against Manchester United in March 2021 and in the home fixture against Manchester City on the last weekend of the campaign.

POSITION: Defender
DoB: 25/03/2002
27. Maisy BARKER

Raised in North Finchley, Lois Joel played for Watford and Arsenal at youth level and was a member of the Chelsea academy side which won the 2016/17 FA WSL Academy League Southern Division title.

Having enrolled at West Virginia University in 2017, she played college soccer for the West Virginia Mountaineers and later turned out for the North Carolina Tar Heels. She joined West Ham United on a short-term contract in October 2020 before signing a one-year deal ahead of the start of the 2021/22 season.

20. Lois JOEL
POSITION: Defender
DoB: 02/06/1999

Experienced Icelandic international midfielder Dagny Brynjarsdottir fulfilled a personal ambition in January 2021, when she signed a one-and-half-year deal with West Ham United - the Club she has supported since childhood.

Brynjarsdottir joined the Hammers from Icelandic side Selfoss, having previously turned out for the likes of Valur, Bayern Munich and Portland Thorns. She made nine Barclays FA Women's Super League appearances in her debut season in Claret and Blue in the second half of the 2020/21 campaign.

32. Dagny BRYNJARSDOTTIR
POSITION: Midfielder
DoB: 10/08/1991

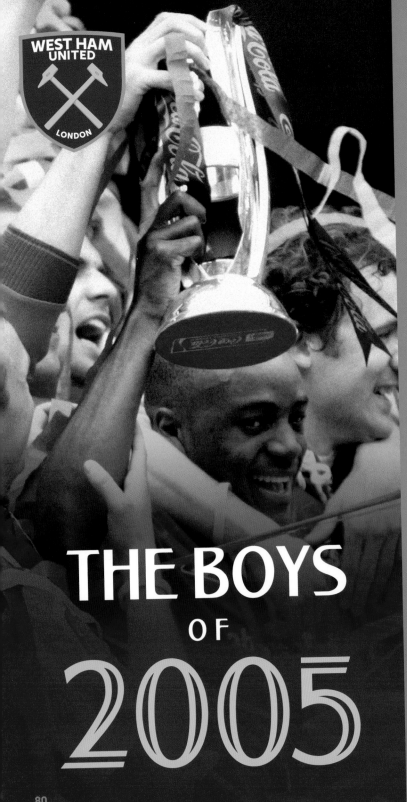

WEST HAM UNITED LONDON

THE BOYS
OF
2005

West Ham United ended a two-season spell in the Championship by securing a return to the Premier League in 2004/05 as Alan Pardew's side successfully navigated the Play-Offs at the second attempt.

After the 2003/04 season ended with the heartbreak of a Play-Off final defeat in Cardiff's Millennium Stadium at the hands of London rivals Crystal Palace, manager Pardew faced the challenge of motivating his troops to go one better the following season. Keen to avoid the lottery of the Play-Off system, automatic promotion was the Hammers' aim and they made an impressive start to their 2004/05 season by winning five of their opening eight Championship fixtures.

A disappointing spell of form in late October and early November saw the Hammers lose touch with high-flying Sunderland and Wigan - the two clubs who would go on to secure the top two spots. Two defeats and two draws in March even threatened the team's bid for a Play-Off place, but a superb run of form at the end of the season saw the Irons secure sixth spot and book a second stab at the Play-Offs.

The Play-Off semi-finals certainly had a feeling of déjà vu as Ipswich Town provided the opposition just as they had done twelve months earlier. Having ended the season in third spot, the Tractor Boys took the advantage of hosting the all-important second leg. Goals from Marlon Harewood and Bobby Zamora saw West Ham race into a two-goal lead in the first leg before Ipswich stunned the Boleyn Ground faithful as they mounted a comeback to draw 2-2.

Ipswich may have had ended the regulation season twelve points ahead of the Hammers, but they froze on the night in front of their own fans and were no match for an exceptional West Ham side that won 2-0 thanks to a second-half brace from Zamora.

Zamora's goals secured the Hammers a 4-2 aggregate success and a return ticket to the Millennium Stadium for the Play-Off final.

As in the 1964 FA Cup, Preston North End were once again West Ham United's final opponents. Unlike the five-goal thriller of 1964, just one goal was enough for the Hammers on this occasion as they sealed their return to the Premier League.

Both Harewood and Zamora threatened early on and Zamora was also frustrated by a goal-line clearance before finally netting the only goal of the game after 57 minutes. West Ham faced a late scare when goalkeeper Jimmy Walker had to go off injured, but substitute Stephen Bywater was not seriously troubled as Pardew's men held on for a priceless win.

MARK NOBLE AND CHRIS POWELL

WEST HAM UNITED LONDON

STAR MAN
MARLON HAREWOOD

Although strike partner Bobby Zamora grabbed the headlines in the latter stages of the season with his Play-Off final winner and semi-final brace, it was Marlon Harewood who ended the 2005/06 campaign as the Hammers leading marksman.

A £500,000 signing from Nottingham Forest in November 2003, Harewood netted 22 goals in all competitions for West Ham United in 2004/05.

A powerful and robust frontman, Harewood's 17 Championship goals proved vital in helping the Irons reach the Play-Offs. He netted both goals in a 2-1 London derby victory over Queens Park Rangers in November 2004 and opened the scoring in an excellent 2-0 pre-Christmas victory away to eventual champions Sunderland. He was also on target in four of the club's final five league games as sixth spot was secured.

MARLON HAREWOOD

BOBBY ZAMORA & ANTON FERDINAND

ELLIOTT WARD & STEPHEN BYWATER

BOBBY ZAMORA CELEBRATES

WEST HAM UNITED

PAGE 20 · HEY REF

1. Direct free kick. **2.** Indirect free kick.
3. Yellow card - Caution. **4.** Red card - Sending off.
5. Obstruction. **6.** Substitution. **7.** Offside/foul.
8. Penalty. **9.** Offside location. **10.** Play on.

PAGE 52 · CLASSIC FAN'TASTIC

Graham Paddon, Trevor Brooking, Pat Holland, Alan Taylor and Mervyn Day.

PAGE 54 · REWIND QUIZ

1. Ipswich Town. **2.** Slavia Prague. **3.** Michail Antonio.
4. Charlton Athletic. **5.** Christian Benteke. **6.** Manuel Lanzini.
7. Darren Randolph. **8.** King Power Stadium (Leicester City).
9. Robert Snodgrass. **10.** Southampton.
11. Stockport County. **12.** One (Tomas Soucek).
13. Manchester United. **14.** Aston Villa. **15.** Jarrod Bowen.
16. Tomas Soucek. **17.** True (v Newcastle United).
18. They won nine Premier League away games in 2020/21.
19. 65 points. **20.** Two (they drew 0-0 with Fulham away).

PAGE 70 · PREMIER LEAGUE QUIZ

1. 2006/07. **2.** Oli Watkins (from Brentford in 2020).
3. 1946/47. **4.** Brentford's new Community Stadium.
5. New Zealand. **6.** Anderlecht. **7.** Manchester City.
8. Michael Keane (v Montenegro). **9.** Eddie Gray (2004).
10. Two (Liverpool and Watford). **11.** Roma.
12. Sergio Aguero. **13.** Brandon Williams (Norwich City).
14. Eight goals. **15.** Alex Neil. **16.** Newcastle United.
17. Norwich City (on loan in 2012/13). **18.** Four (Javi Gracia, Quique Flores, Hayden Mullins twice and Nigel Pearson).
19. Ian Wright. **20.** Matt Jarvis (in 2011).